CURLICUE
Kinetic Origami
Assia Brill

Curlicue - Kinetic Origami

Copyright © Assia Brill 2013
Origami models, Diagrams, Text, Photographs by Assia Brill

All rights reserved. No part of this publication may be reproduced
or utilised in any form or by any means, electronic or mechanical,
including photocopying, recording, or by any information storage
and retrieval system, without prior written permission from the author.

The origami models in this book may not be used for commercial
purposes without written permission from the author.

ISBN-13 978-1494234935
ISBN-10 1494234939

Preface

The Curlicue
was born in 2005
after a few experiments
with *Palaspas* palm leaf strips.

It is a new type of moving or kinetic origami.
You can rotate the Curlicue's stacked layers
to reveal fascinating, constantly changing patterns
of radiating stars and zigzag spirals.

It's not difficult to fold the model, even though it looks
quite complicated. It's simply formed by repeated valley
folds, without turning over the paper.

I've chosen to defy tradition by first showing a method for
folding the Curlicue which isn't the simplest. This is for two
reasons:
- Accuracy. It's vital for the folds to be very precise.
  This is achieved by the first method.
- Enjoyment. The twisting manoeuvre is fascinating and fun,
  and I want you to experience it.

I've done my best to explain this first method as clearly
as possible, but you may find it a bit difficult. In this
case you can resort to a simpler method which is not
quite so accurate and may be less enjoyable.

I'm a perfectionist. I'd like you to obtain the best
possible results too! The keys to success are:
- Use thin but strong paper, with good colour
  contrasts between faces.
- Cut the strip very accurately, making
  sure it has straight, sharp, evenly
  tapering sides.
- Fold very precisely,
  lining up the edges
  of the strip
  exactly.

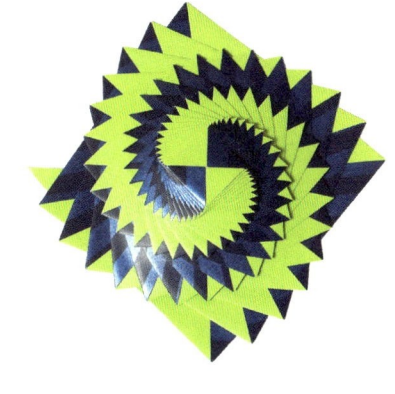

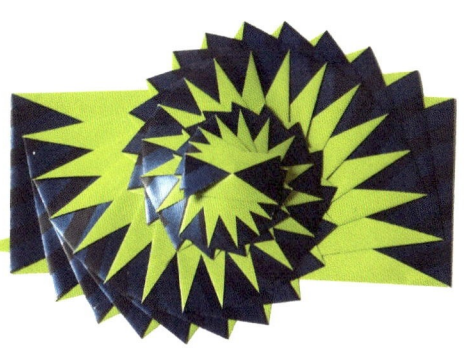

Contents

Preface	1
Contents	2
Symbols	4

CHAPTER 1 Single Strip Square Curlicues	7
The Curlicue	8
Square Curlicue: The Twist Fix	10
Curlicue. Mountain Fold method	12
Let's Twist Again! Playing with Curlicue	15
Dancing Curlicues	17
Prism Curlicue	19

CHAPTER 2 Double Square Curlicues	21
Double Curlicue 1	23
Double Curlicue 2	24
Double Curlicue 3	25
Double Prism Curlicue	26
Double Prism Curlicue 1	27
Double Prism Curlicue 2	28
Double Prism Curlicue 3	29

CHAPTER 3 Hexagonal Curlicues	31
Hexagonal Curlicues	33
Single Strip Hexagonal Curlicues	34
Prism Hexagonal Curlicue	34
Hexagonal Curlicue	35
Double Prism Hexagonal Curlicue	37
Double Hexagonal Curlicues	39
Double Hexagonal Curlicue	40
Hexagonal Curlicue: The Twist Fix	42
Securing the two strips	46
Simple Connection Start	47
Simple Connection Finishes	48
Single Lock Start	50
Single Lock Finishes	52
Double Lock Start	54
Double Lock Finish	55

CHAPTER 4 Rectangular Curlicues	57
Rectangular Curlicue 45°	58
Prism Rectangular Curlicue 60°	59
Double Rectangular Curlicue 45°	60
Double Prism Rectangular Curlicue 45°	62
CHAPTER 5 Fun Models	65
Cushioned Coaster	66
Puzzle Coaster	68
CHAPTER 6 Easy ways to cut tapering strips	71
Some helpful tips	72
Acknowledgements	76
Postscript	78

Symbols

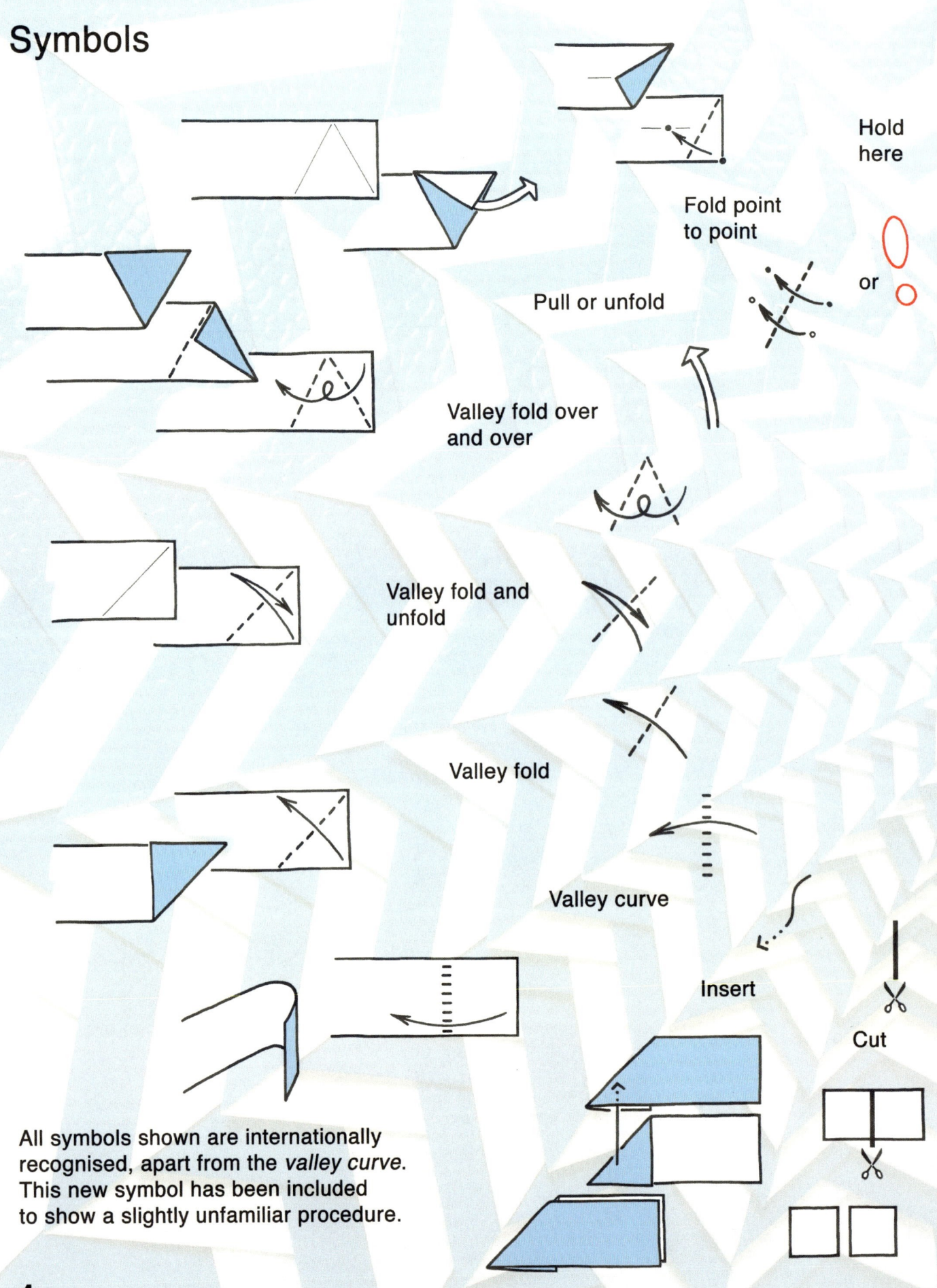

All symbols shown are internationally recognised, apart from the *valley curve*. This new symbol has been included to show a slightly unfamiliar procedure.

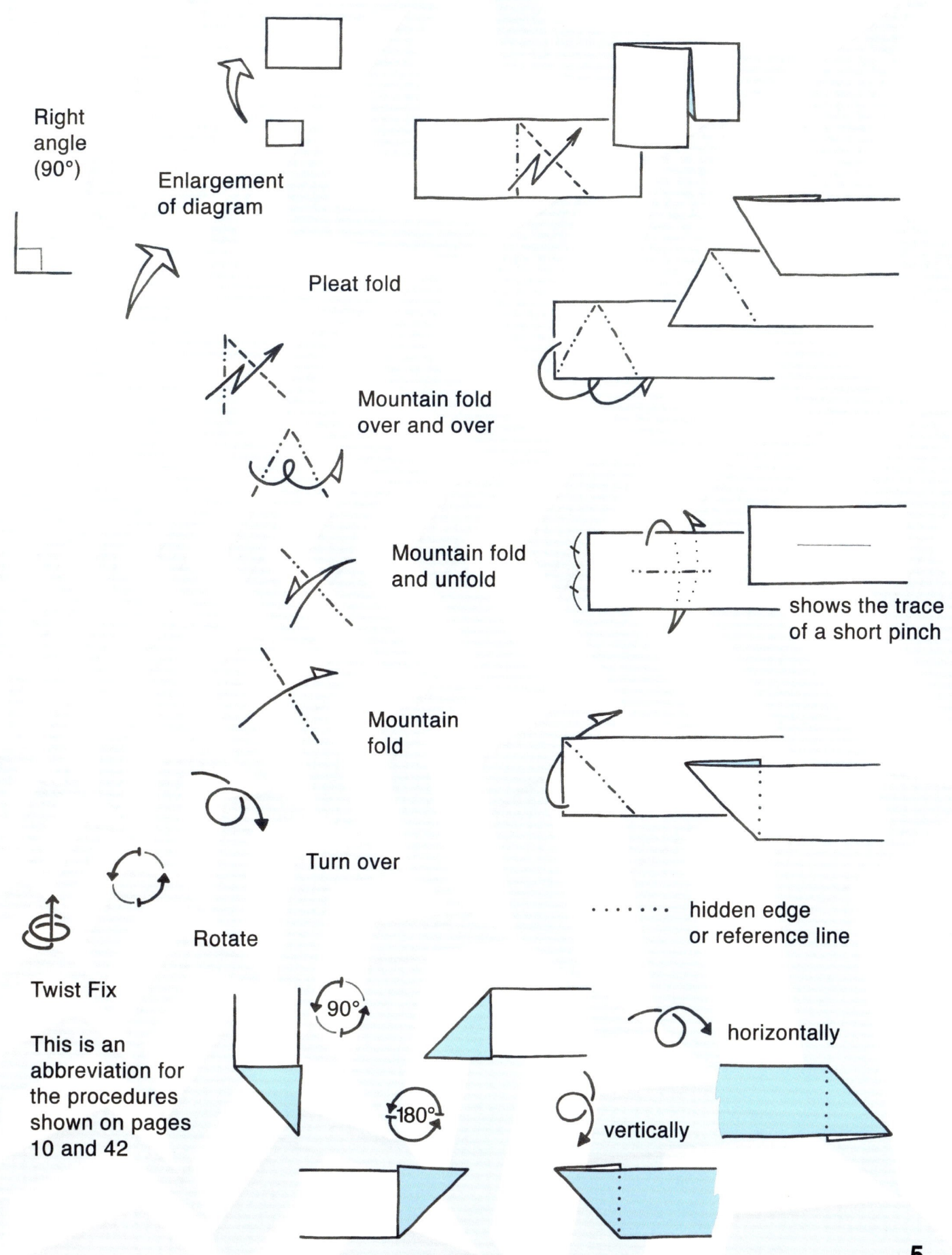

Single Strip Square Curlicues

The Curlicue

This Curlicue is folded from a tapering strip. The strip can be of any length, but the longer the better. To practise, try a short strip first. I recommend one measuring 30 x 5 x 1 cm cut from coloured wrapping paper, or from a sheet of A4.

Here, and throughout the book, you will find that not all steps have accompanying notes.

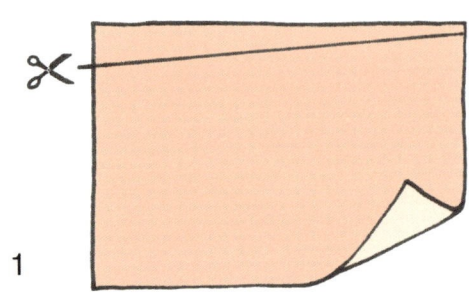

1

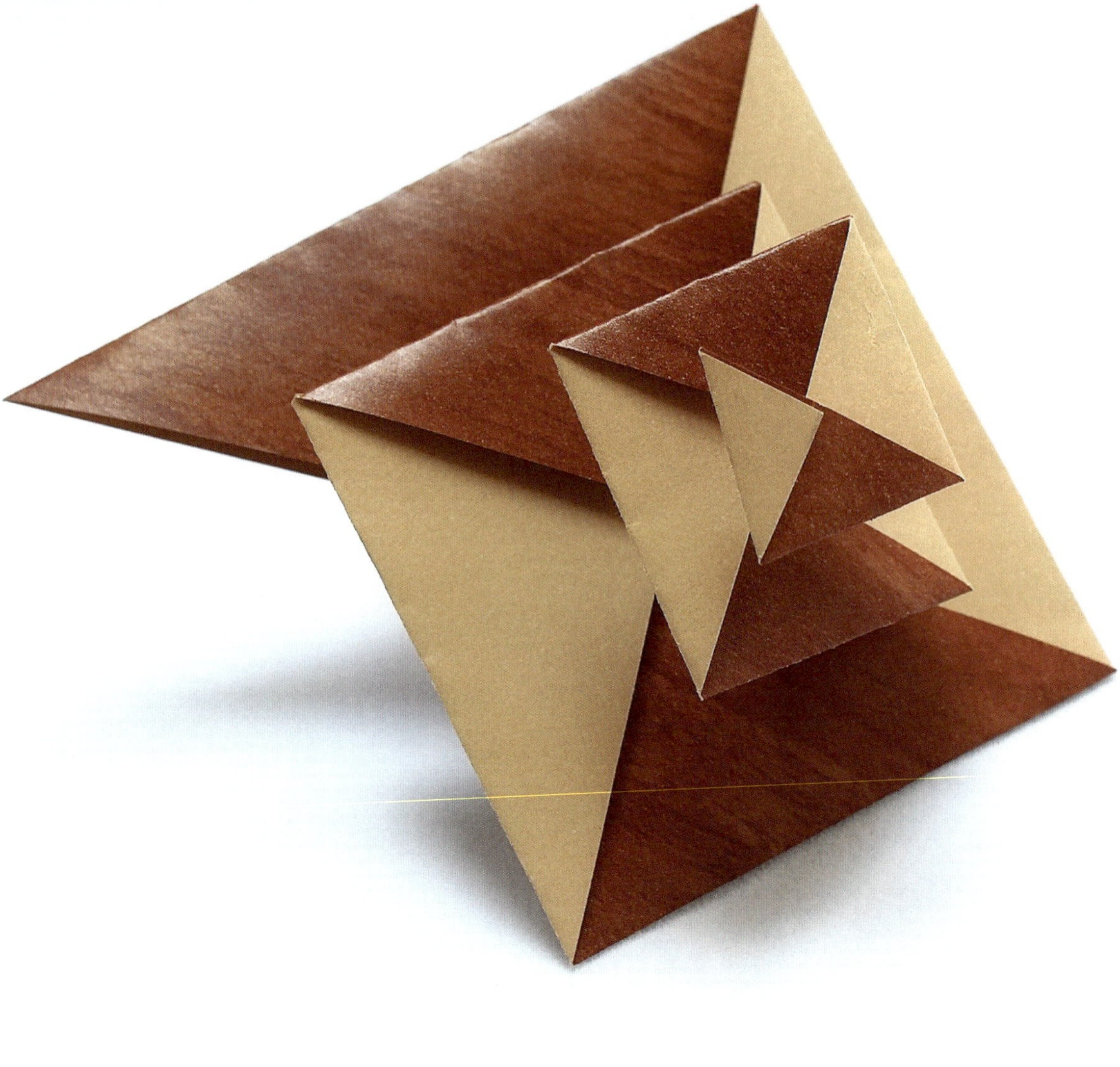

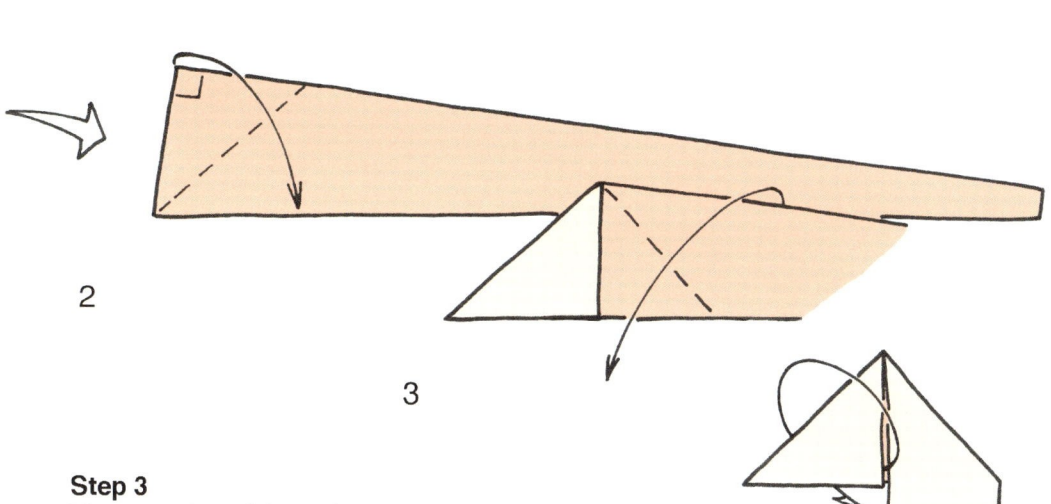

Step 3
The top edge of the strip is valley folded to lie along the vertical edge. Ensure that a sharp corner is obtained at the top.

Continue along the strip, repeating the valley folds using the same principle. Fold very precisely, checking that the corners always lie on diagonal axes.

You will find it easier to rotate the paper anticlockwise after each fold, so that you are in the best position to make the next fold precisely. The free end of the strip is then always positioned on the right horizontally, as in steps 3 and 8. For clarity the diagrams don't always show it this way. Once you are familiar with the process of course you can choose your own method.

When you run out of paper at the end of the strip, cut the end along the horizontal or vertical raw edge underneath. Do not cut diagonally!

Step 9
The folding has been done by the *Valley Fold Method*. The model appears to be ready, but we have a loose paper spiral: if you pull the ends, the spiral will come undone. We need to lock the spiral with a special procedure - the *Twist Fix*, see page 10.

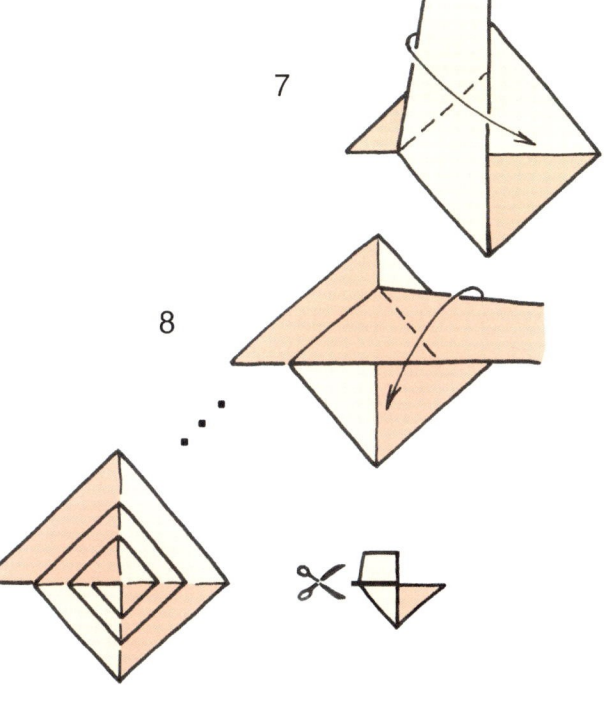

Twist Fix for Square Curlicue

This symbol is shown wherever the Twist Fix is required.

This twist manipulation is unusual in origami. Instead of hard creases you should make gentle curves in the paper. No new folds are needed: in fact, they should be avoided.

Imagine your hands when opening a jar when viewed from above, the hand holding the lid makes an anticlockwise movement, and the hand which holds the jar moves clockwise. The Twist Fix is similar.

The twisting process consists of inverting the layers one by one, continuing down the spiral. Begin with the top layer. As you work, the layers you have completed are locked together and move anticlockwise (the lid), while the remaining loose ones move clockwise (the jar). When you reach the wider end of the spiral, all is firmly fixed.

Between the locked and loose sections, there is always a soft valley curve (see photos).
In the diagrams a valley curve symbol IIIII indicates this.
Remember, it's a smooth curve, not a hard fold.

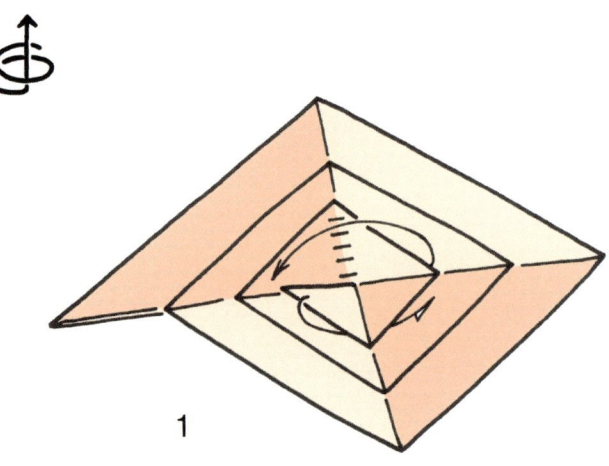

1

Step 2
The position of the hands is very important: two fingers of the left hand hold all the layers except the uppermost one, two fingers of the right hand hold one corner marked by the red ring. The right hand is omitted from the drawings for clarity.
Rotate this corner 180° anticlockwise around the central vertical axis.

Step 3 onwards
Reposition your hands and repeat the rotation. Notice that as you lock a new layer, the right hand will grasp an additional corner and the locked layers will increase in thickness.

Important!
During the twisting process, don't stretch the spiral and don't pull or displace the layers. Instead think of an imaginary thread passing through the central vertical axis, which holds together all the layers to stop this from occurring.

I love this manoeuvre! I hope you will too, when you get the hang of it.

Continue until all the layers are locked, see step 10. Job done! The Curlicue is finished.

Now you've succeeded, try another one from a longer tapering strip.

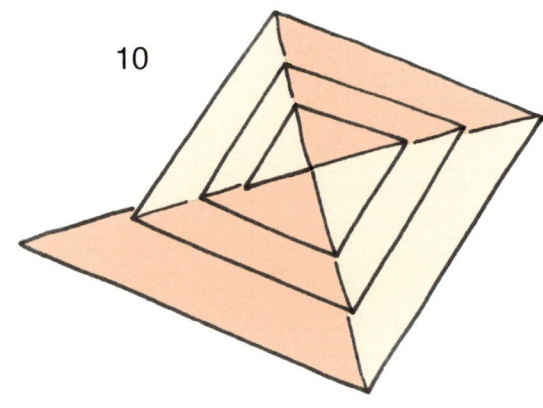

10

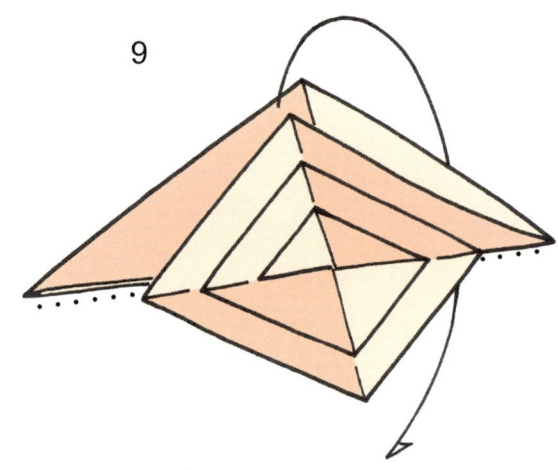

9

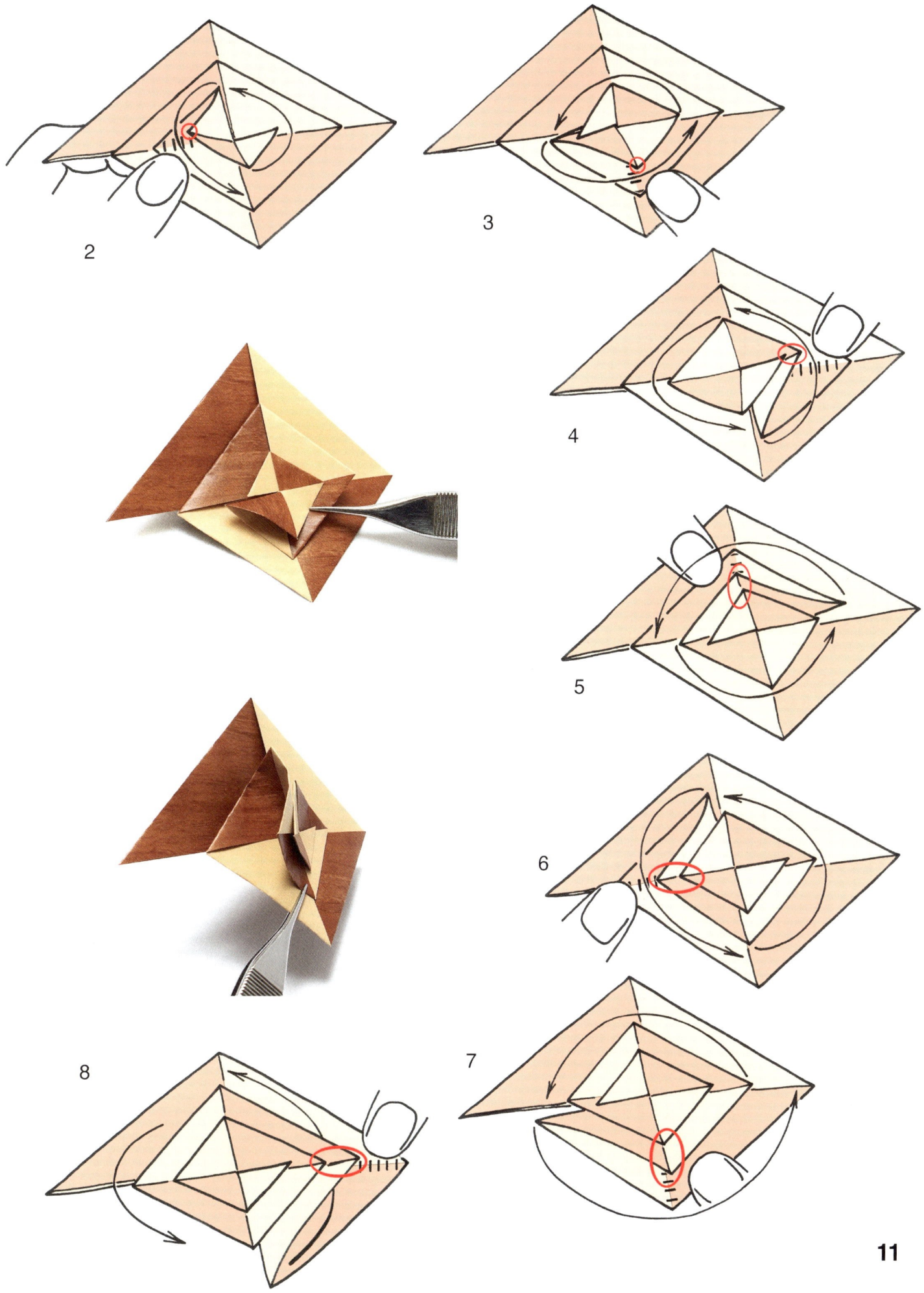

Twist Fix: some tips

If you experience difficulty making the Twist Fix, have a look at page 42 for a description of a similar Twist Fix for the Hexagonal Curlicue, which has been drawn from a slightly different viewpoint. This may clarify the process. As a last resort, please try the simple method below.

Curlicue
Mountain Fold method

It's possible to fold the Curlicue omitting the Twist Fix, page 10. The spiral will be fixed automatically.
You can start here with a brand new strip, or continue with the folded strip which you used before. Unfold your pre-creased spiral (step 9, page 9) and start from step 1 below.

After step 6 all folds are made as mountain folds instead of valley folds.

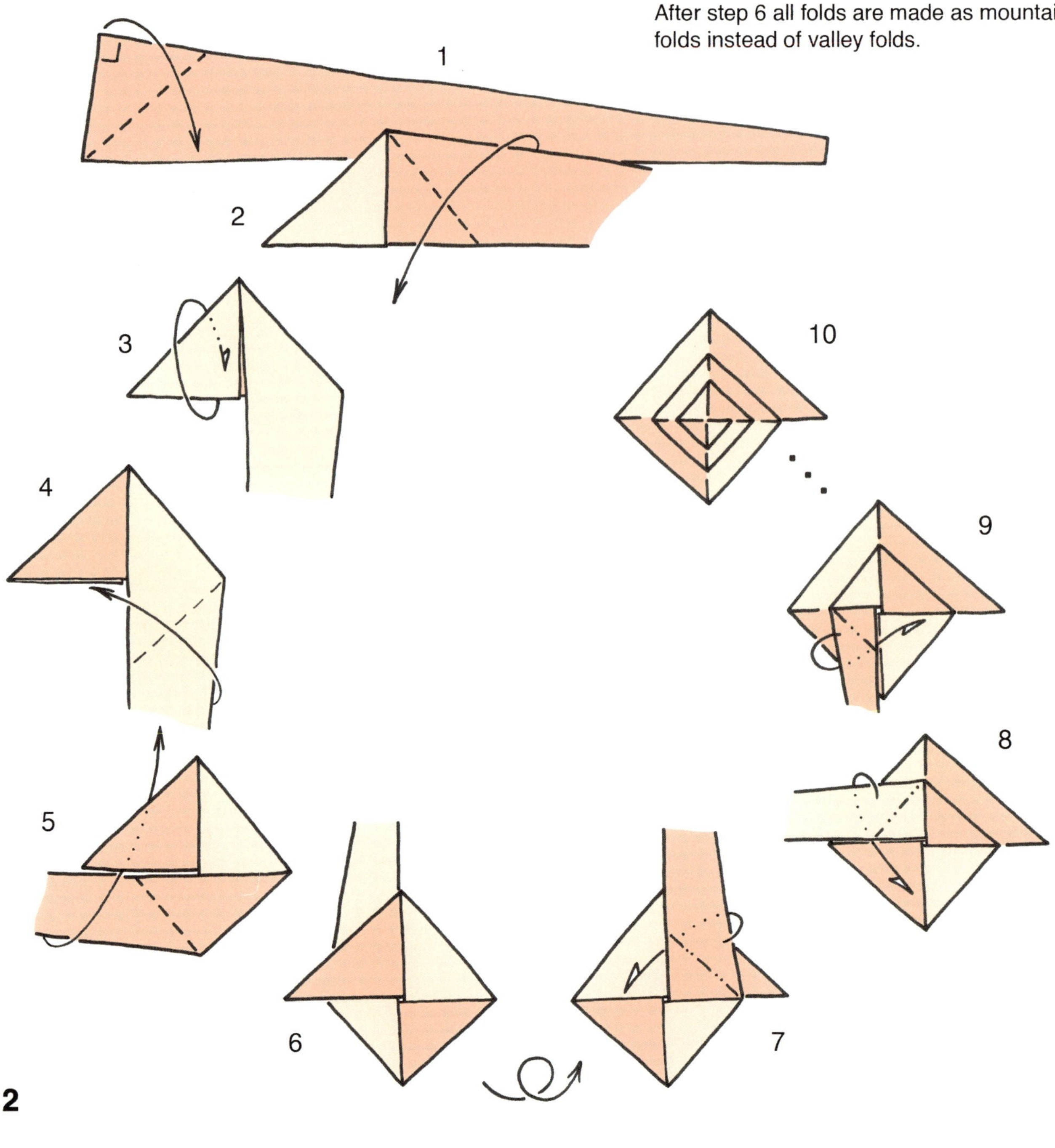

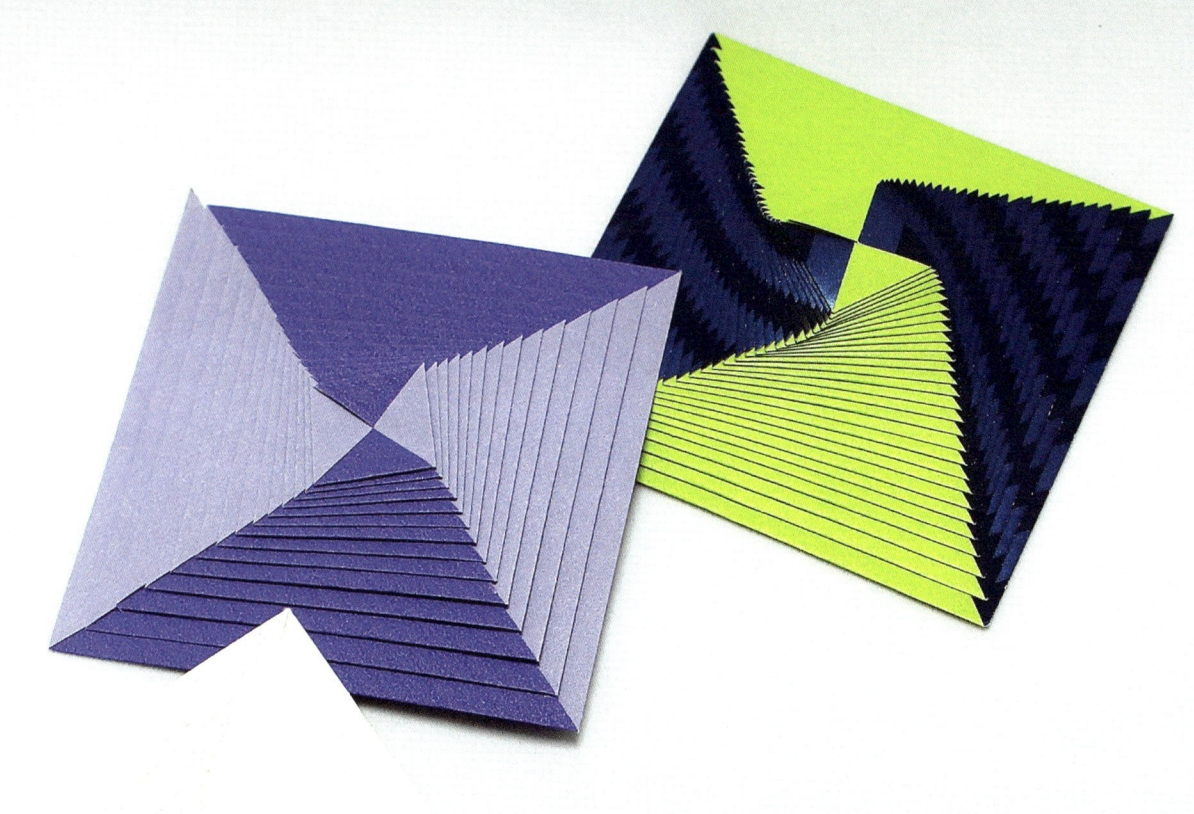

Let's twist again! Playing with the Curlicue

Now you can enjoy the Curlicue's kaleidoscopic patterns. Holding the Curlicue with both hands as shown (1), begin to rotate the layers anticlockwise by pushing the corners of the squares lightly with your thumbs.
The magic begins as striking patterns emerge, transforming into stars and whirling spirals as you continue the rotation.

As you twist the Curlicue, line up the "spokes" radiating from the centre to form symmetrical patterns. With each small rotation you'll discover different arrangements. It's up to you now to explore and experiment!

The formation of patterns continues as you twist. The Curlicue begins to take many three-dimensional shapes, including a triangular pyramid (3), a curvy flattened cone (4), and eventually a pointed tree-like shape (5). At all stages the colour arrangements are intriguing and almost inexplicable…

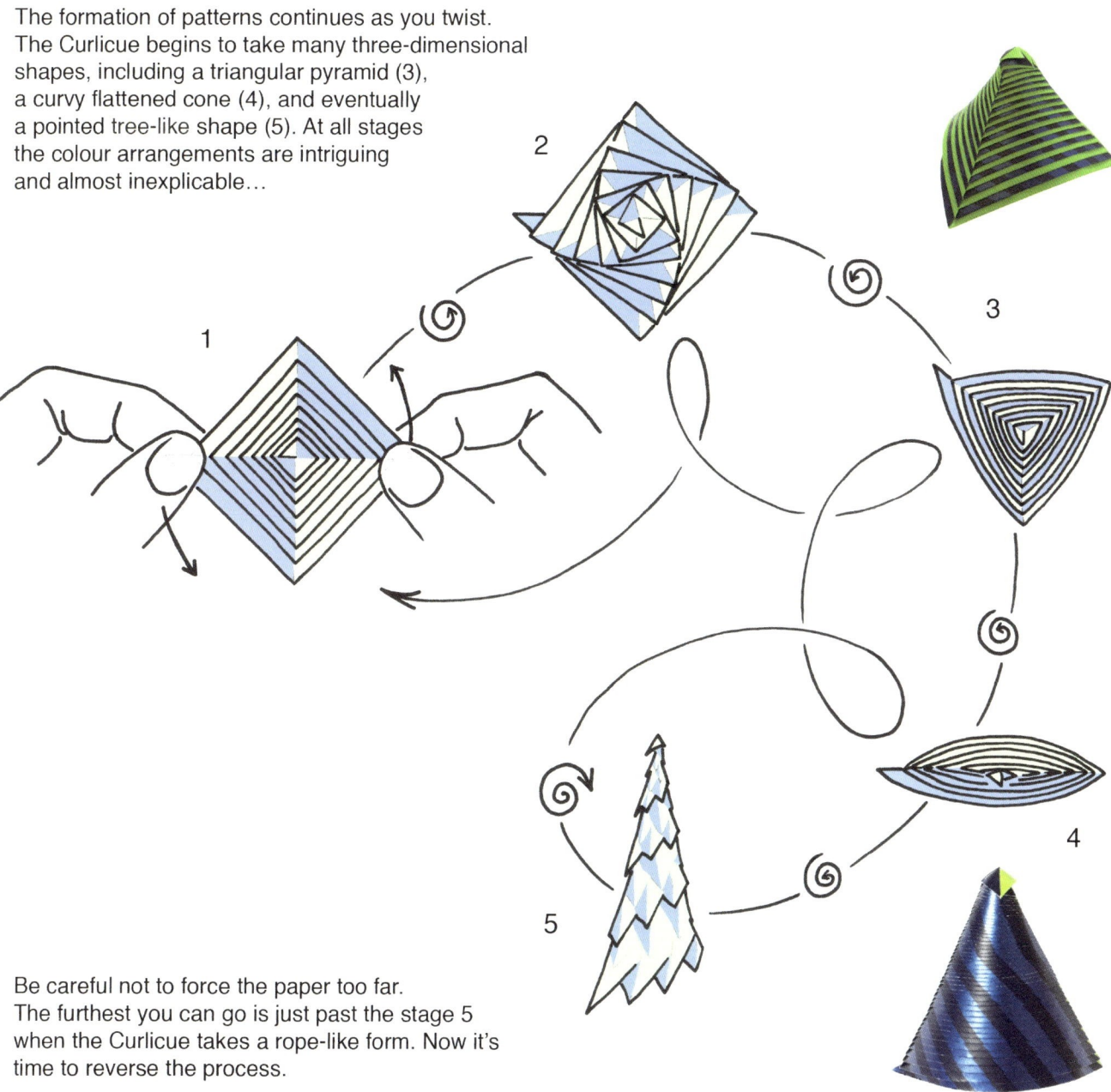

Be careful not to force the paper too far. The furthest you can go is just past the stage 5 when the Curlicue takes a rope-like form. Now it's time to reverse the process.

Begin by untwisting, rotating the layers clockwise. Take care at the two sided cone (4) and three sided pyramid (3) stages, because raw edges between the layers tend to lock together. Unlock them carefully, starting from the upper layers, separating and releasing the pressure between them, and rotating gently clockwise.

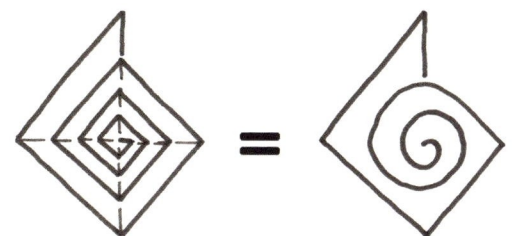

Dancing Curlicues

This Curlicue variation uses paper of one colour (e.g. green both sides). Make several Curlicues of the same size, in different colours, using the diagrams on pages 8 to 11.
Now they need to be connected by interlacing.

Step 1
Place two Curlicues side by side as shown, and lift half of each Curlicue gently.

Step 2
Connect them by sliding together as shown.

Step 3
Begin interleaving the two spirals. As they intertwine, they seem to be dancing together.

The finished spiral is beautiful in itself, but you can play with it as shown on page 15 to produce new patterns.

It is possible to interlace the Curlicues in other ways too, e.g. back to back, or with three or four Curlicues. I leave it to your ingenuity to experiment!

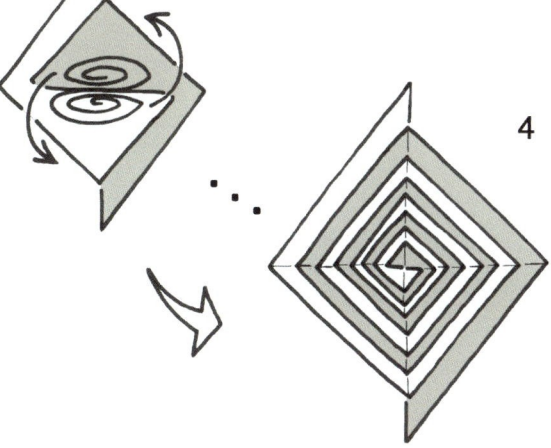

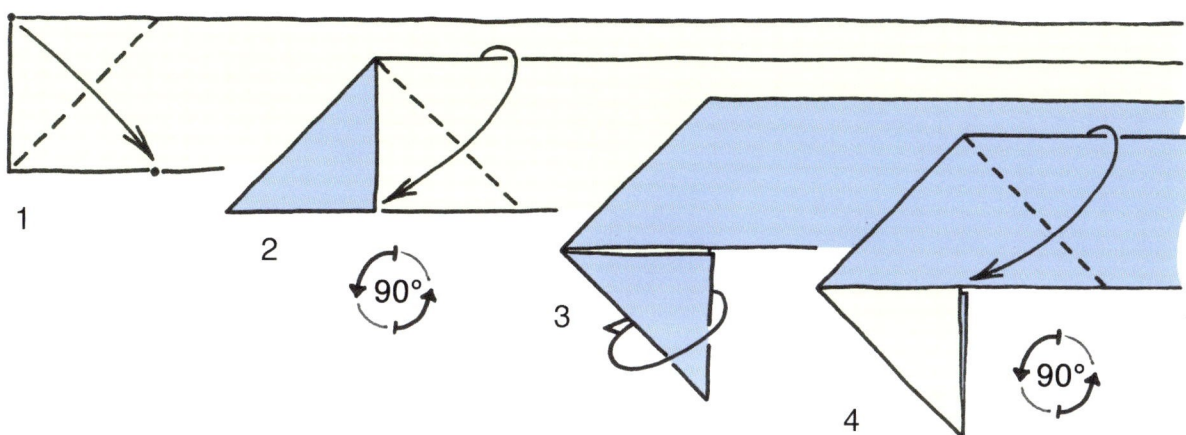

Prism Curlicue

A Curlicue made from a parallel strip resembles a square-based, multi-layered prism. The longer the starting strip, the taller the completed prism.

The folding process is simple and repetitive. First make a diagonal valley fold, then rotate the model, making an anti-clockwise quarter turn. Fold once more, then rotate, and so on. Although seemingly simple, this Curlicue is tricky to fold because the reference points are hidden, unlike the tapering strip version where the reference points are clearly visible. So take your time!

When made from a very long strip, the pattern of sides of the prism "tower" forms dramatic spiral shapes when twisted. Made from non-adhesive decorative plastic tape, it will last a long time.

Step 6
Cut off the end and lock the loose spiral with the Twist Fix shown on page 10.

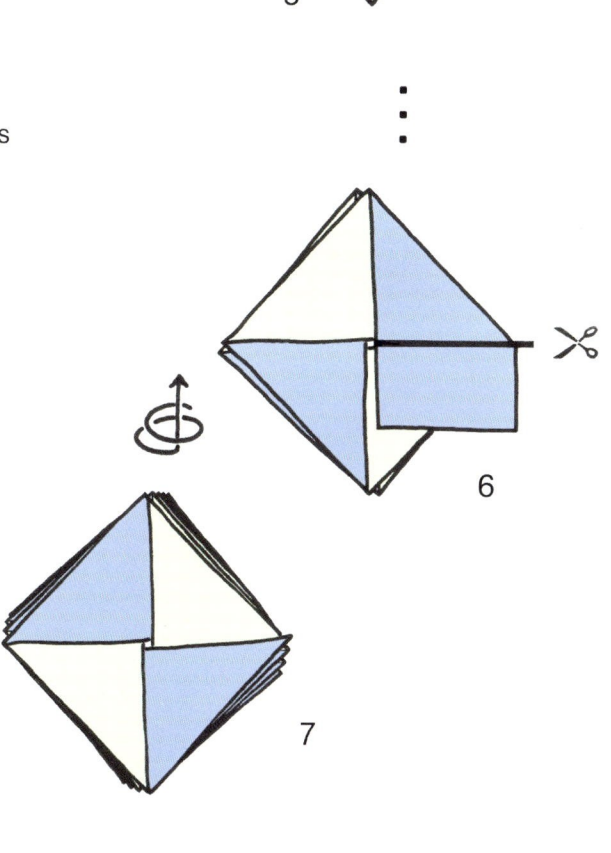

19

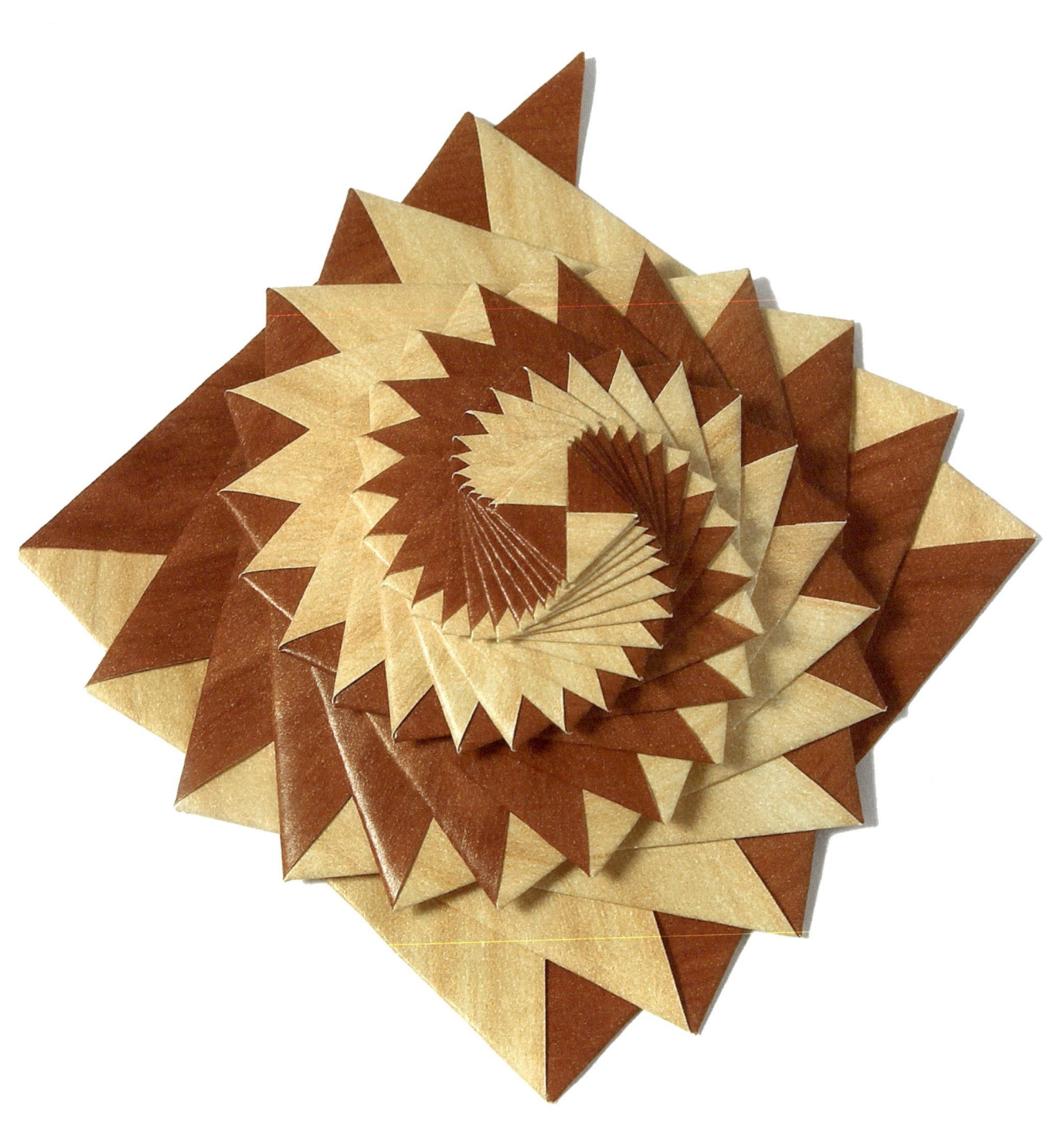

2

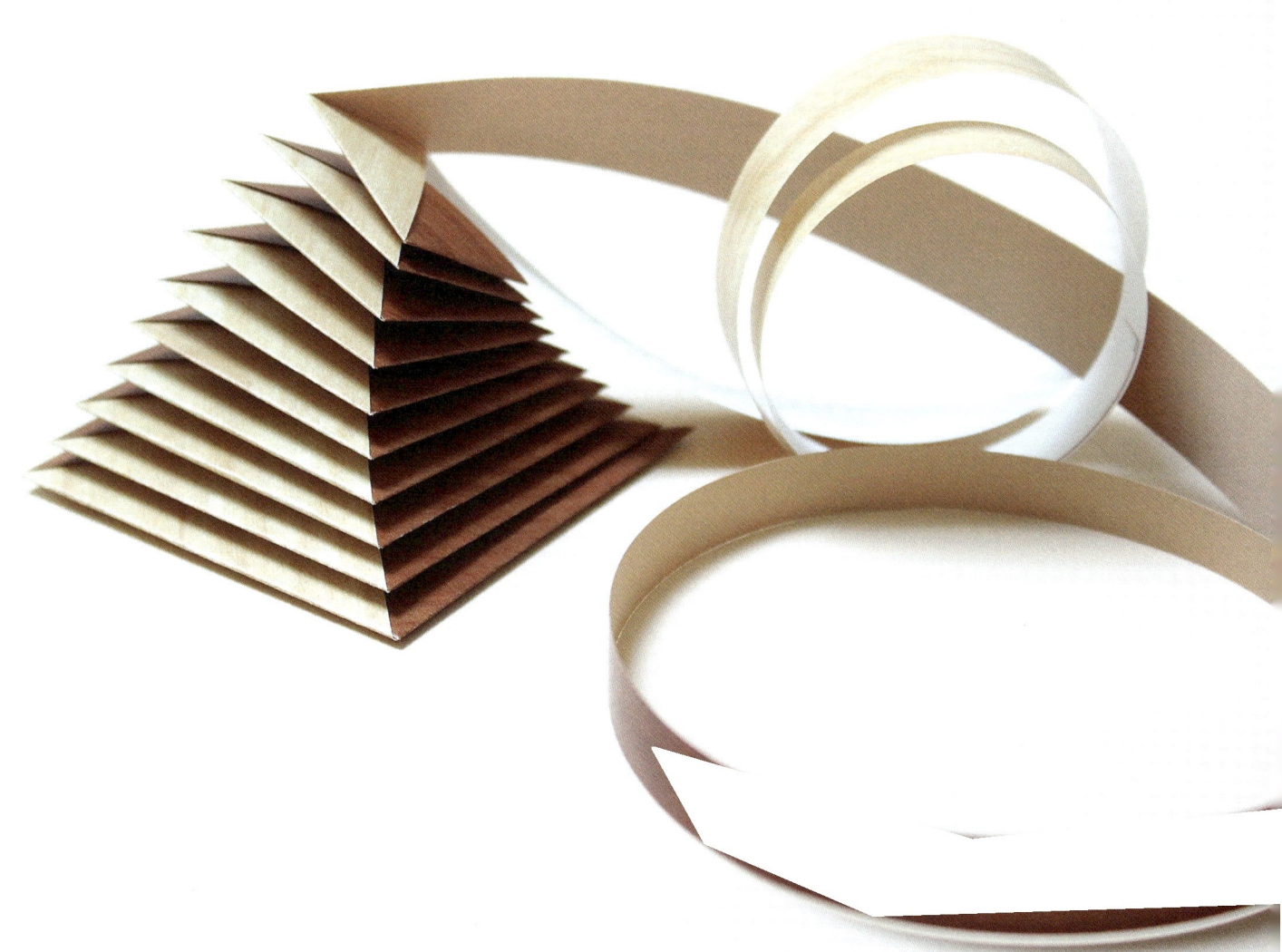

Double Square Curlicues

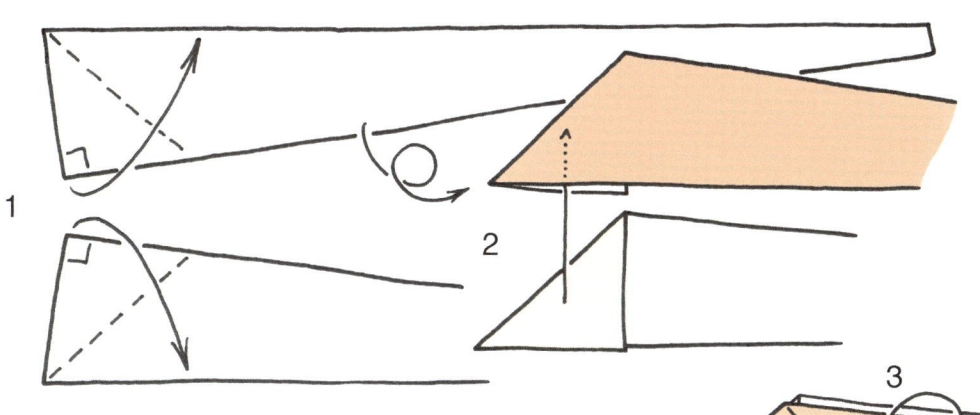

Double Curlicue 1

The Double Curlicue is made from two interwoven tapering strips. It's thicker and stronger than the basic Curlicue. Therefore, you can choose specific colour combinations.

Note that each valley fold for the basic Curlicue (page 9, step 3) is equivalent to two folds (a mountain fold *and* a valley fold) for the Double Curlicue (step 3 and 4, step 5 **a+b**).

Step 6
Cut both layers of the strip.

Finish the Double Curlicue with the Twist Fix procedure shown on page 10. You may find this more difficult because of the extra layers, but the technique is the same as for the basic Curlicue.

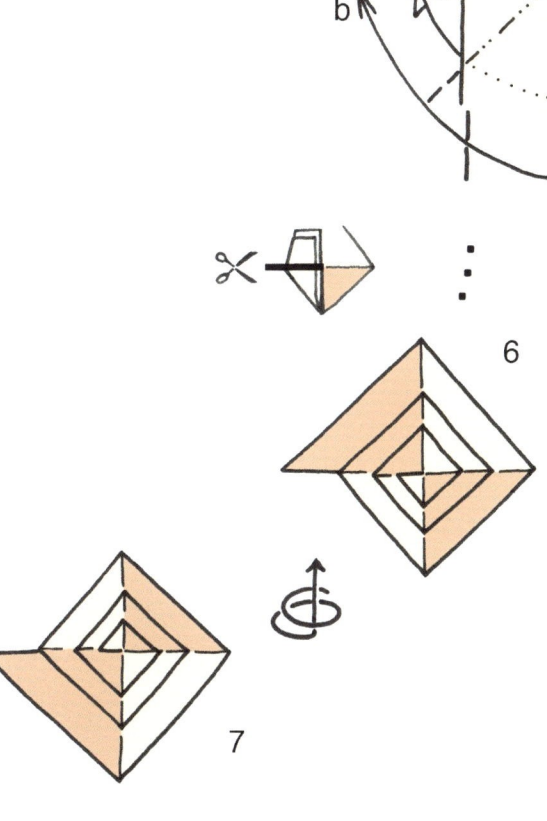

23

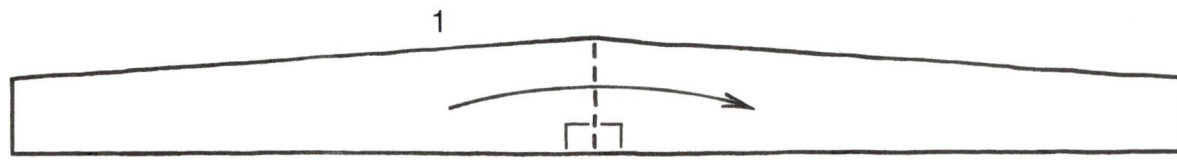

Double Curlicue 2

This is a single colour Curlicue folded from one double tapering strip, wide in the centre and narrow at each end. Note that the lower edge of the strip is a straight line.

Step 4
Continue folding from step 3 on page 23.

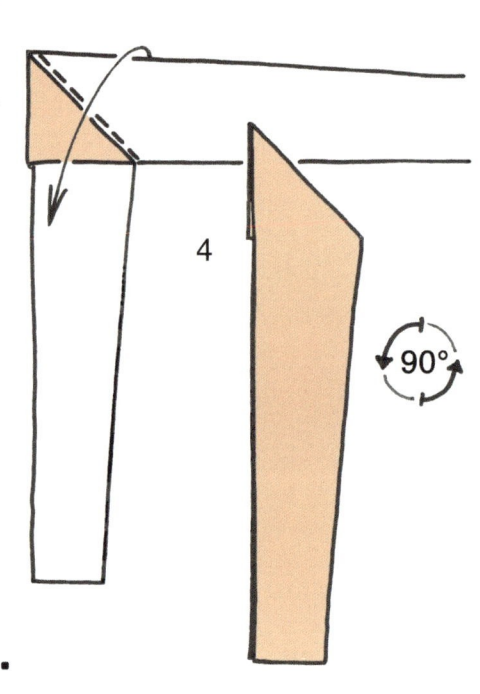

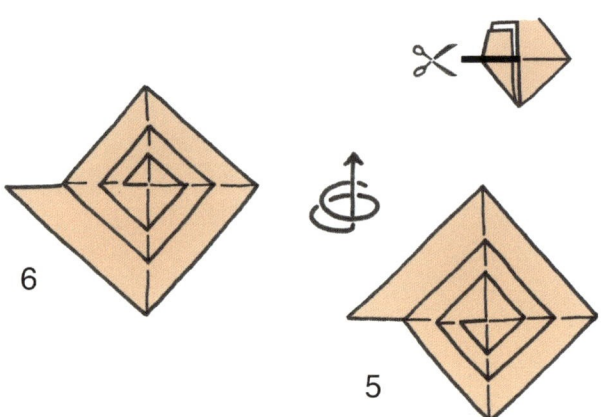

24

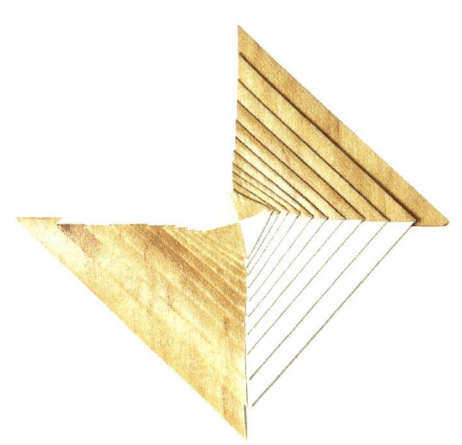

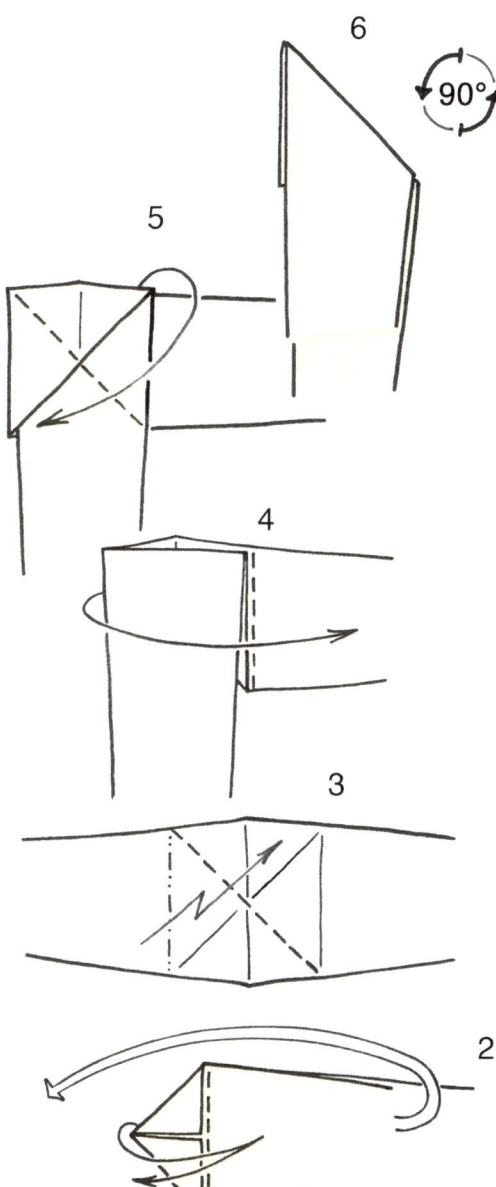

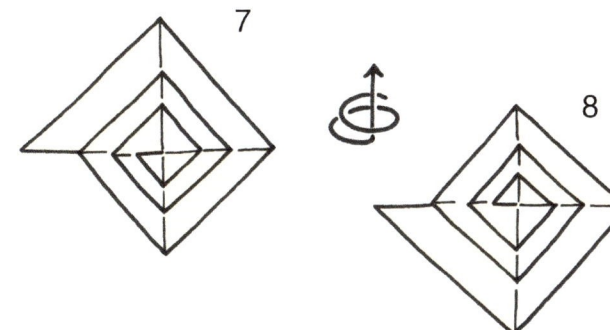

Double Curlicue 3

This is similar to Double Curlicue 2, but uses both sides of the paper to give a colour change. Note that the strip is wide in the centre, tapers towards each end and neither edge of the opened strip is a straight line.

Step 2
After making the valley fold, unfold completely.

Step 3 and 4
Use the creases already prepared in steps 1 and 2.

Step 6
Continue folding from step 3 on page 23.

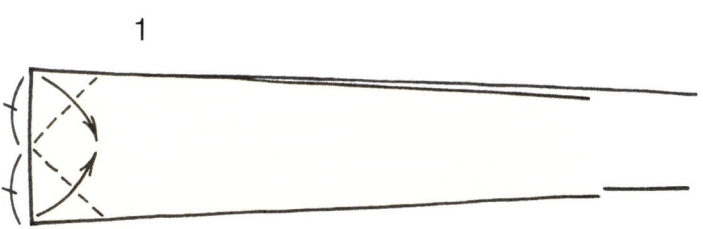

25

Double Prism Curlicue

This is made from two interwoven parallel strips, and is similar in appearance to the Prism Curlicue on page 19. As for the Double Curlicue, there are three variations:

- *Two colour* Double Prism Curlicue from two strips.
- *Single colour from one strip*, folded in half.
- *Two colour from one strip*, folded in half and turned over.

Double Prism Curlicue 1

Use two parallel strips of different colours.
After step 9 continue to repeat steps 7 to 9, i.e. mountain fold, valley fold, rotate. Ensure that the initial 45° corner formed in step 3 is always under the new layers.

Finish with the Twist Fix procedure shown on page 10.

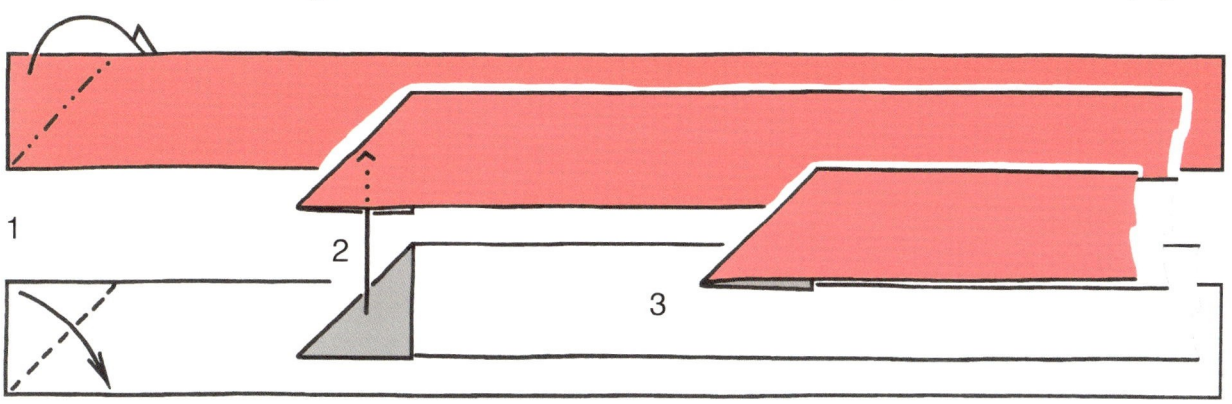

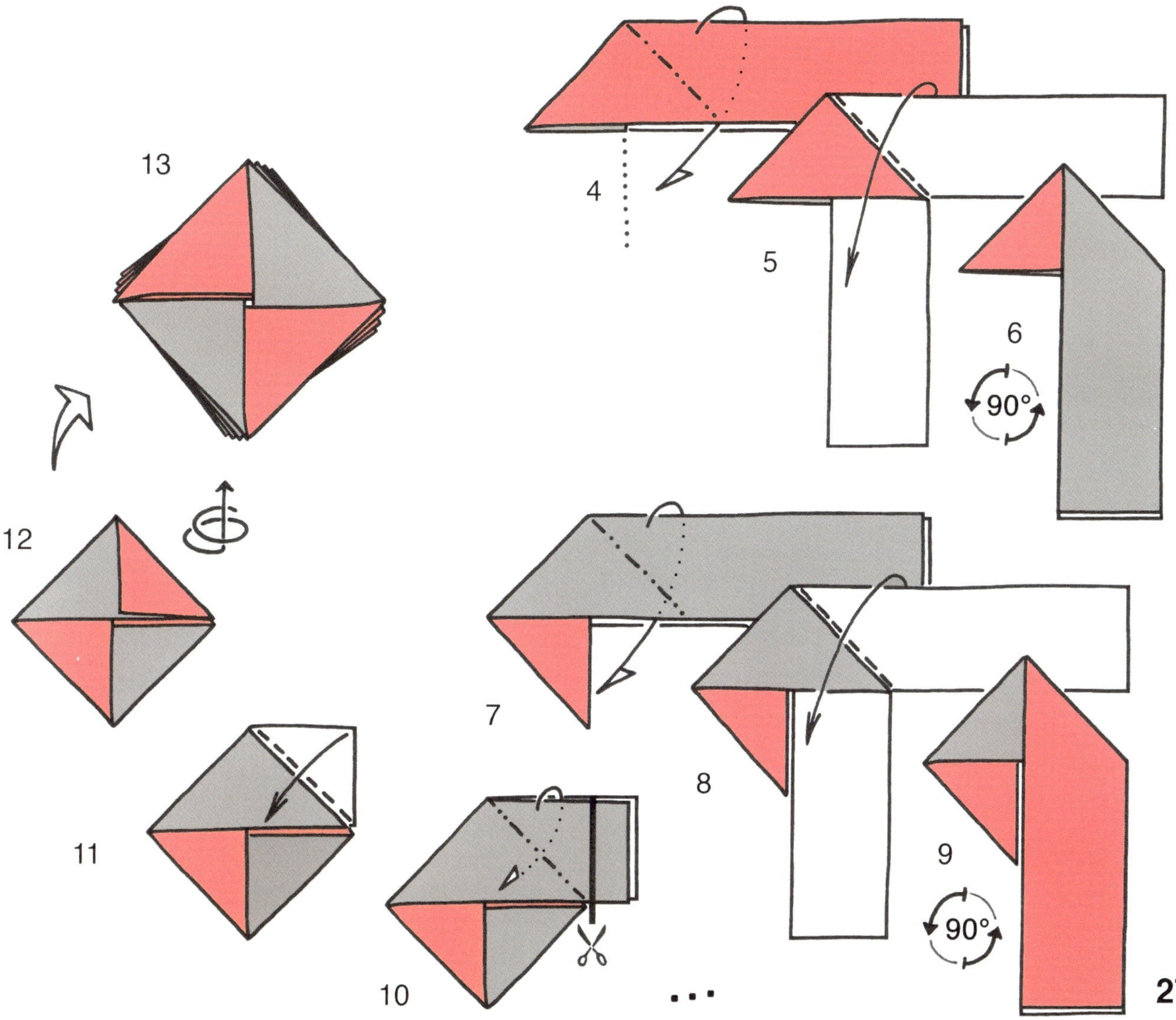

27

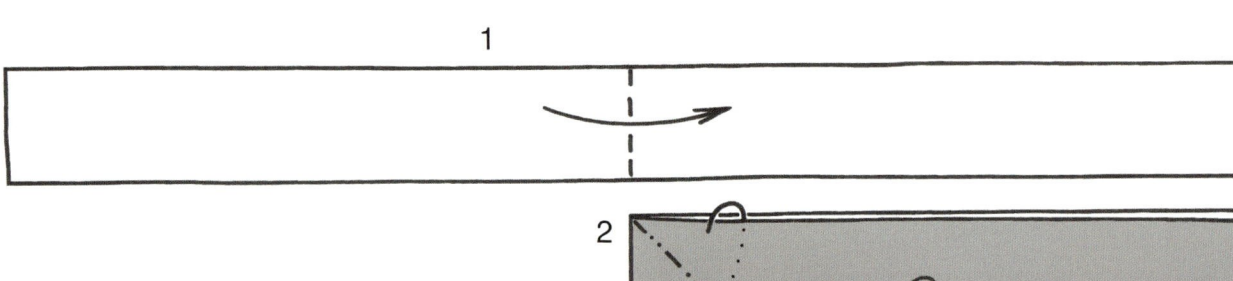

Double Prism Curlicue 2

Follow the procedures from the previous variation. Continue from step 4 on page 27.

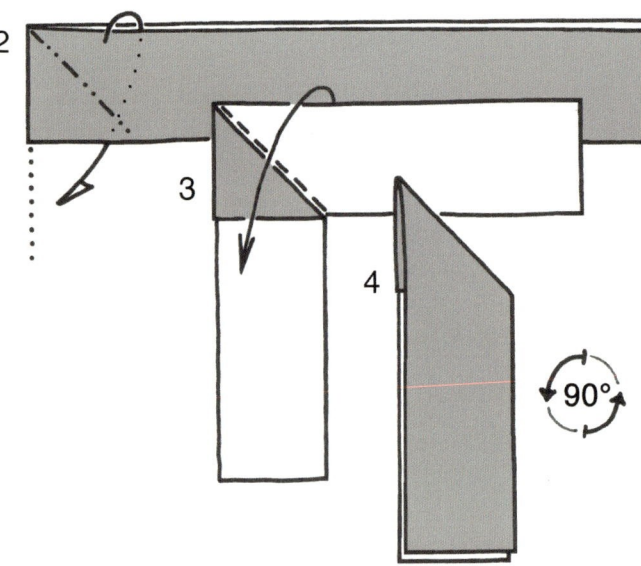

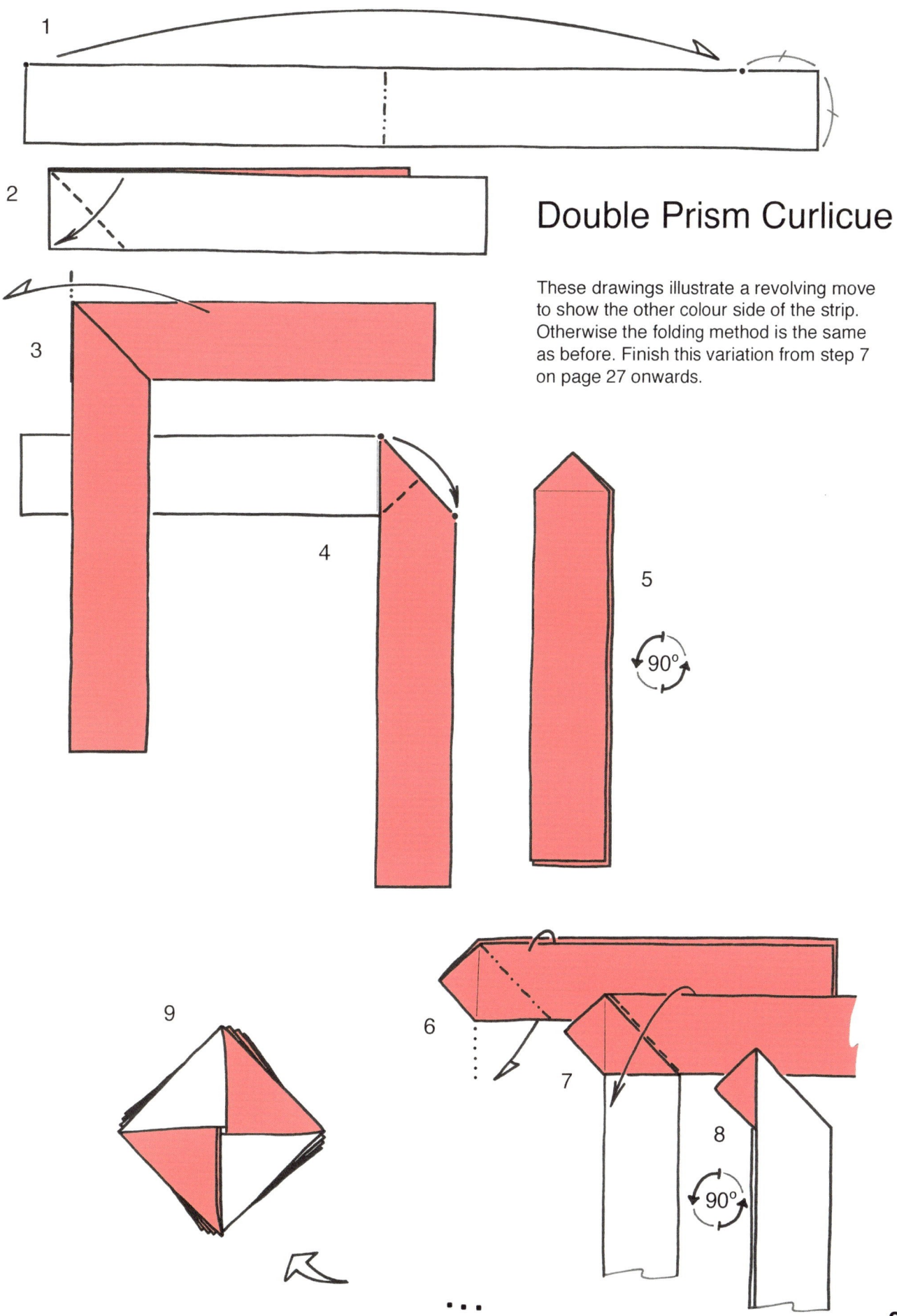

Double Prism Curlicue 3

These drawings illustrate a revolving move to show the other colour side of the strip. Otherwise the folding method is the same as before. Finish this variation from step 7 on page 27 onwards.

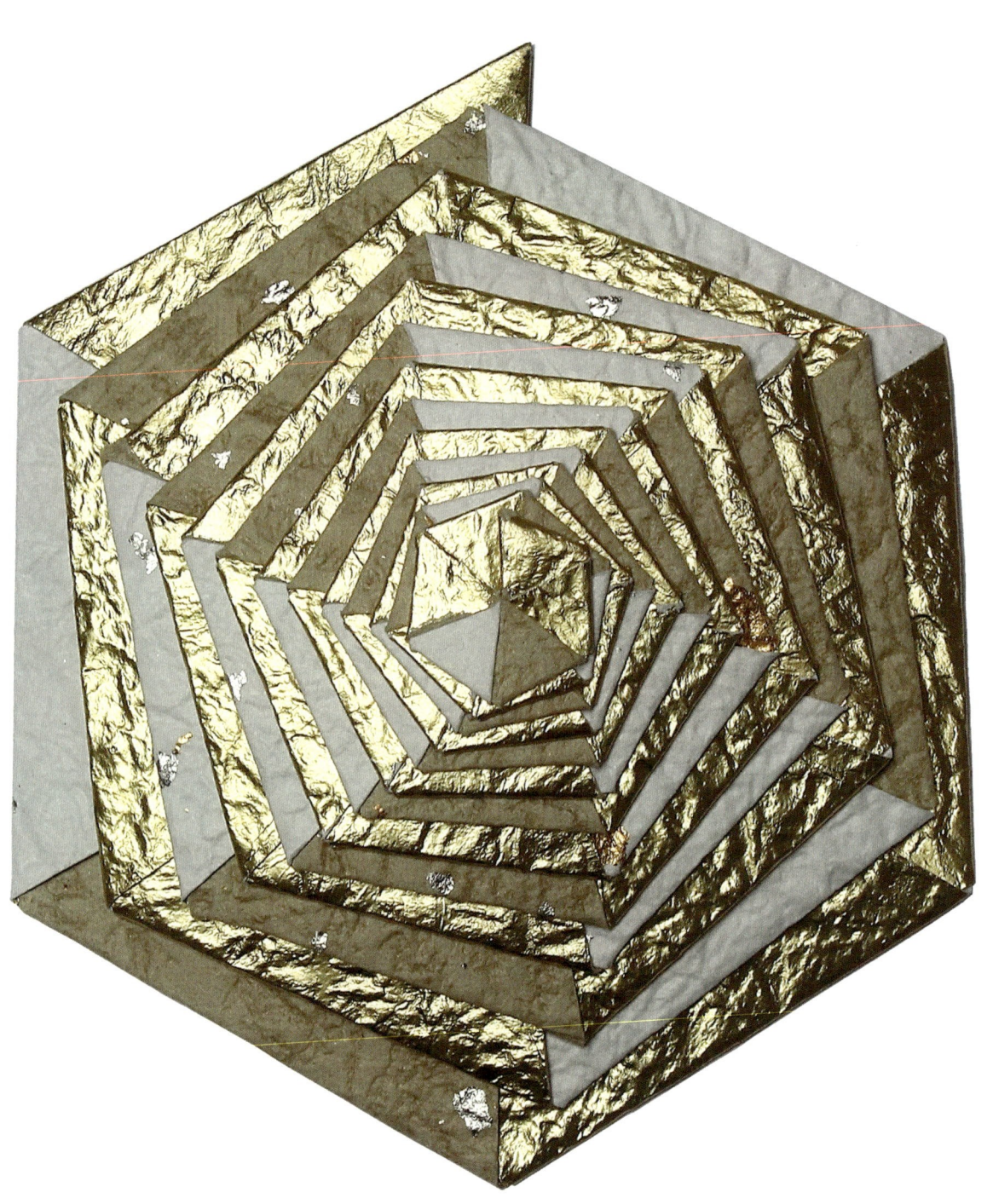

3

Hexagonal Curlicues

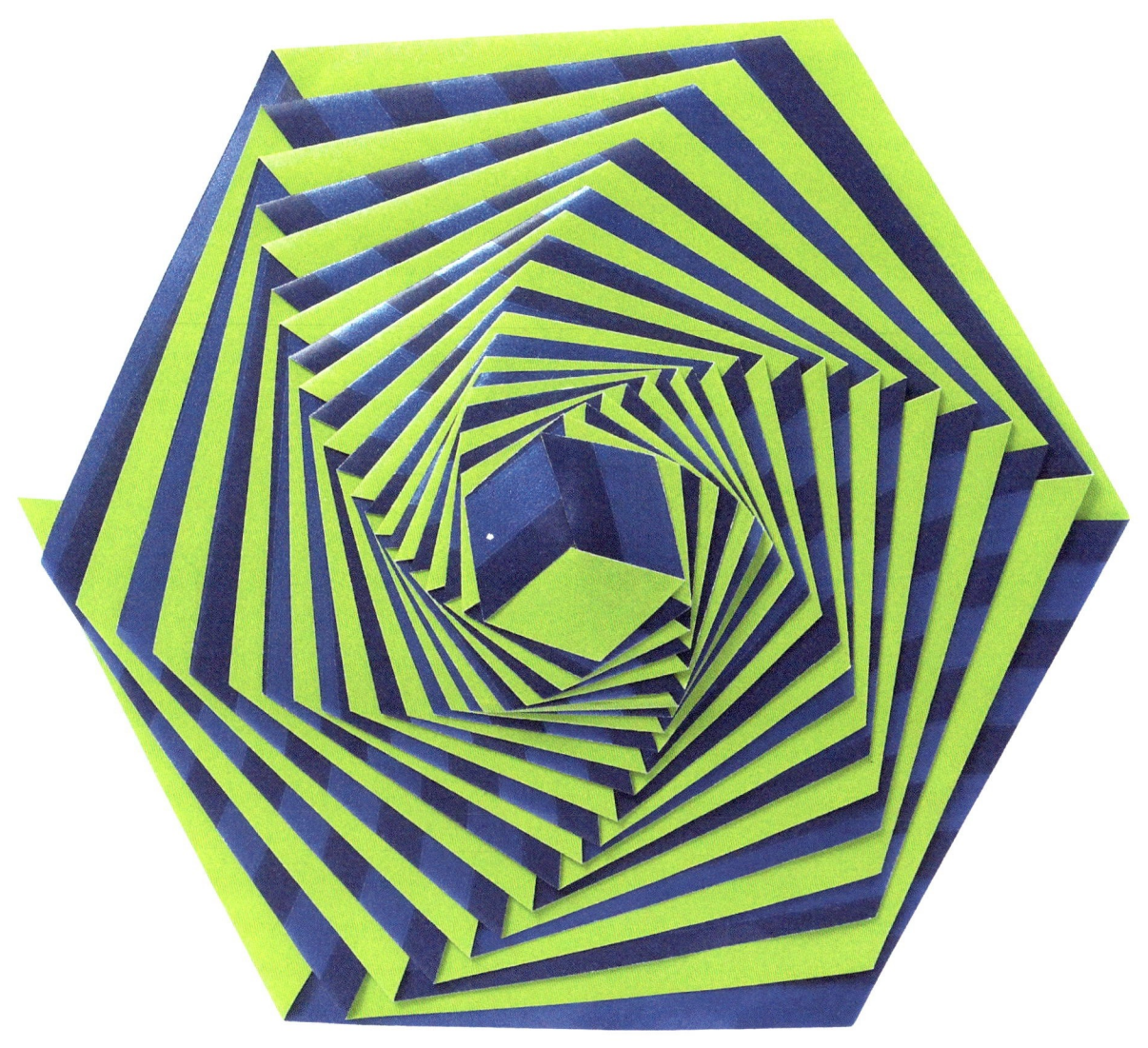

Hexagonal Curlicues

After experimentation with the basic square curlicue, the next step was to try with other geometries: triangular, pentagonal and hexagonal. So far I have only succeeded with the hexagonal variation.

Like the square curlicue, the hexagonal version can be folded from **parallel** or **tapering** strips, in each case using either two interwoven strips, or a single strip. However the single strip version is very fragile and less easy to manipulate. This is because the layers are distributed unevenly: the six "sectors" of the hexagon alternate between single and double layers. The outside edges of the hexagon similarly alternate between raw and folded edges.

Single Strip Hexagonal Curlicues

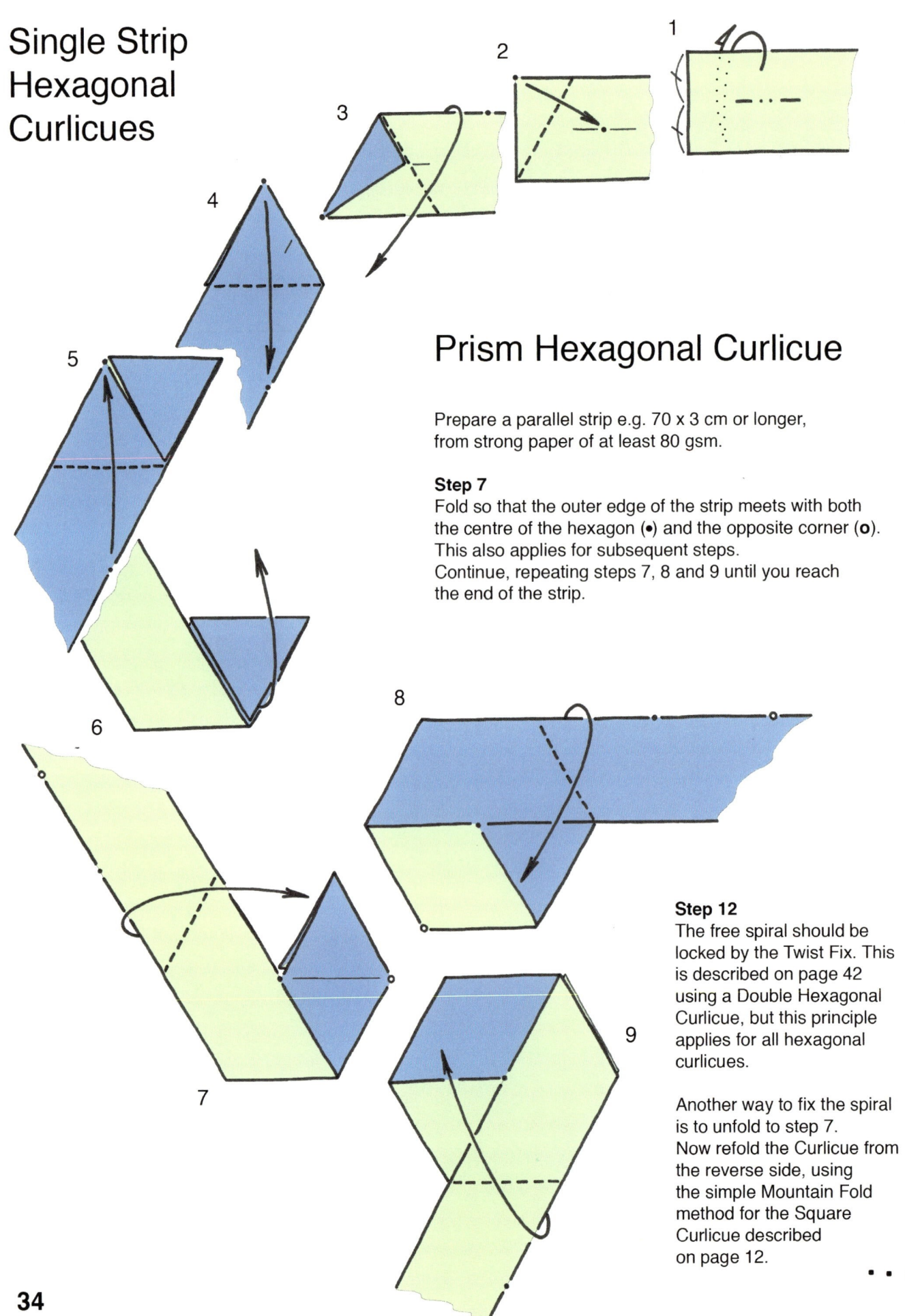

Prism Hexagonal Curlicue

Prepare a parallel strip e.g. 70 x 3 cm or longer, from strong paper of at least 80 gsm.

Step 7
Fold so that the outer edge of the strip meets with both the centre of the hexagon (•) and the opposite corner (o). This also applies for subsequent steps.
Continue, repeating steps 7, 8 and 9 until you reach the end of the strip.

Step 12
The free spiral should be locked by the Twist Fix. This is described on page 42 using a Double Hexagonal Curlicue, but this principle applies for all hexagonal curlicues.

Another way to fix the spiral is to unfold to step 7. Now refold the Curlicue from the reverse side, using the simple Mountain Fold method for the Square Curlicue described on page 12.

. . .

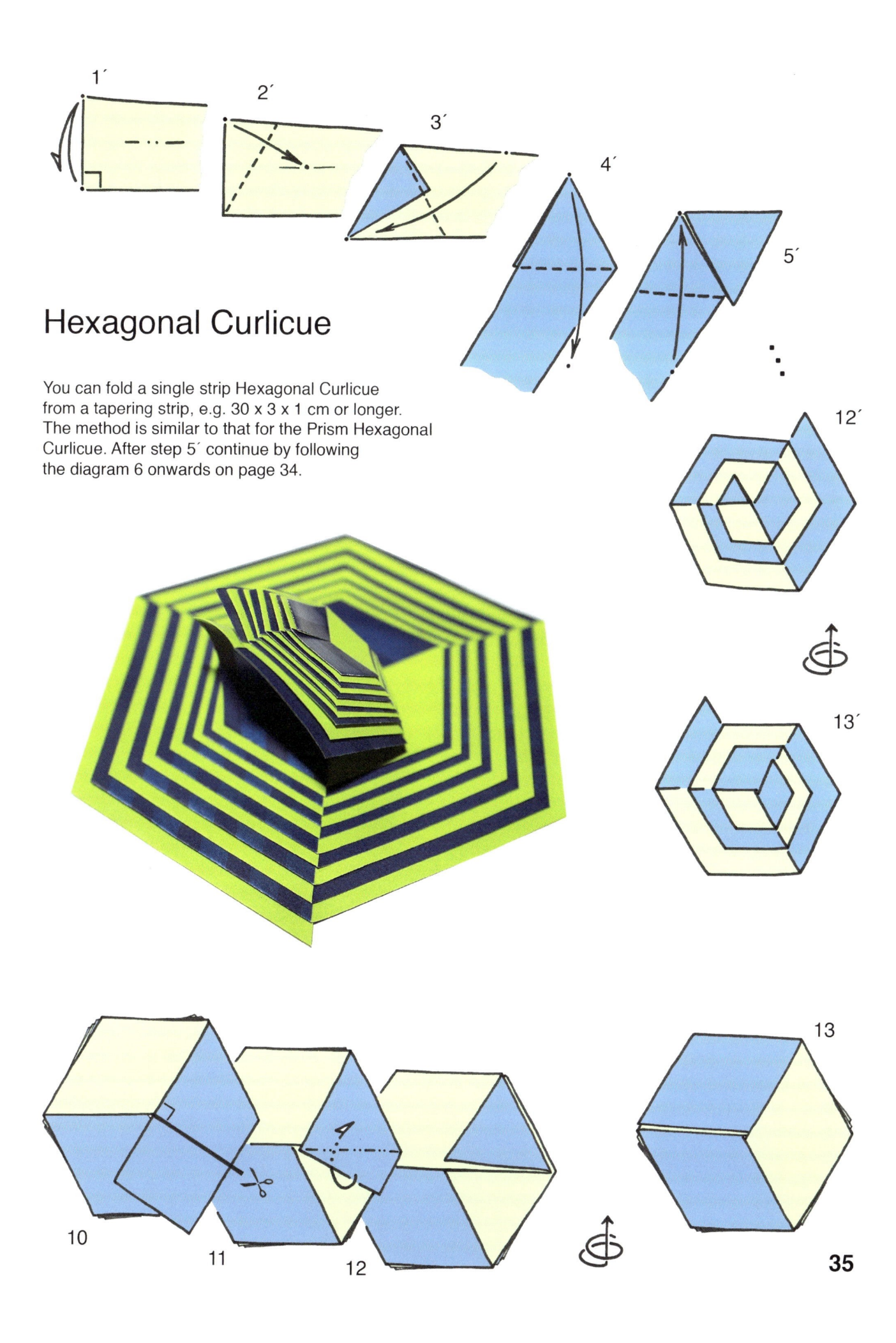

Hexagonal Curlicue

You can fold a single strip Hexagonal Curlicue from a tapering strip, e.g. 30 x 3 x 1 cm or longer. The method is similar to that for the Prism Hexagonal Curlicue. After step 5´ continue by following the diagram 6 onwards on page 34.

35

8

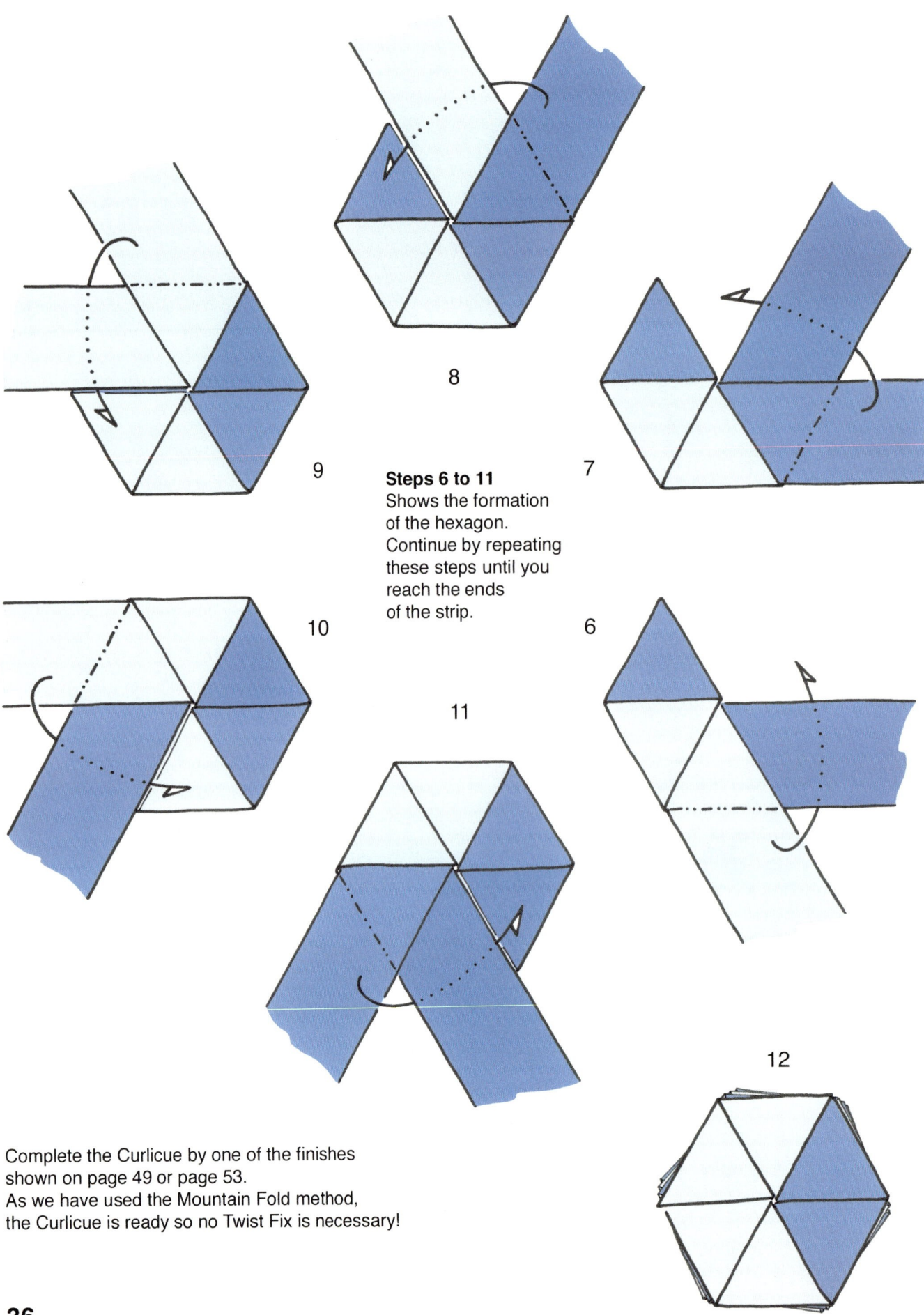

9

Steps 6 to 11
Shows the formation of the hexagon. Continue by repeating these steps until you reach the ends of the strip.

7

10

6

11

12

Complete the Curlicue by one of the finishes shown on page 49 or page 53.
As we have used the Mountain Fold method, the Curlicue is ready so no Twist Fix is necessary!

36

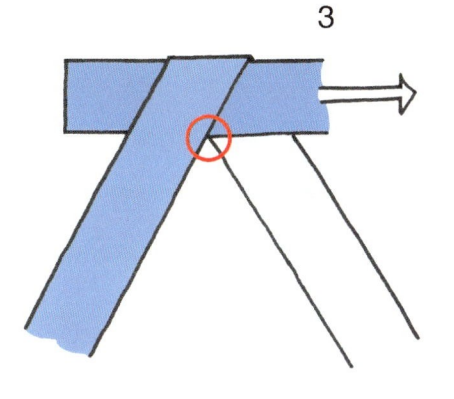

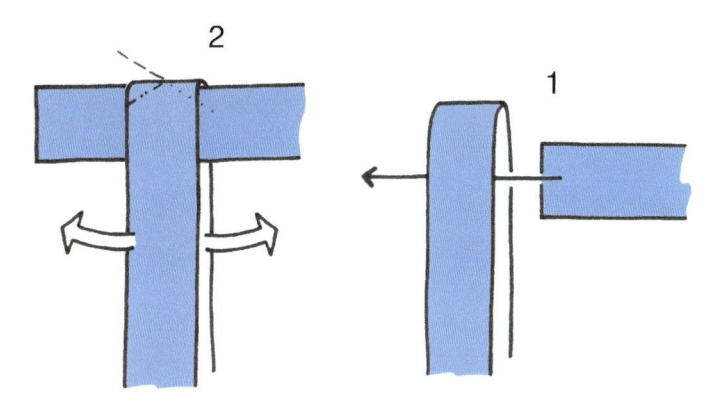

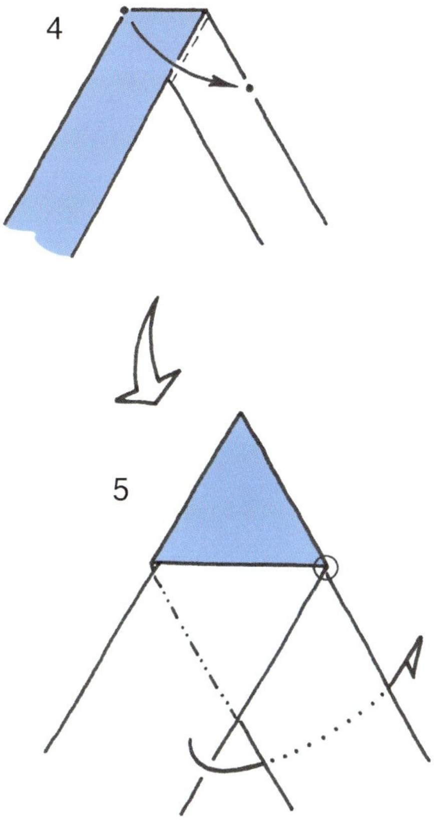

Double Prism Hexagonal Curlicue

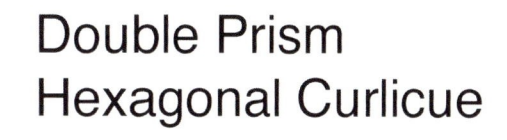

Start with one parallel strip, e.g. 70 x 2 cm or longer.

Step 1
Fold in half softly: the fold doesn't need to be exactly in the centre of the strip. Temporarily insert one loose end of the same strip between the layers.

Step 2
Swivel the two front and back layers to the left and right as shown.

Step 3
Precision is vital to obtain a perfect 60-degree angle! To do this, ensure that:
a) the upper creased edge of the long strip lies tightly on the horizontal edge,
b) all three edges coincide exactly at the circled point.

Step 5
Fold so that the outer edge of the strip touches the circled point: this will be the centre of the hexagon.

37

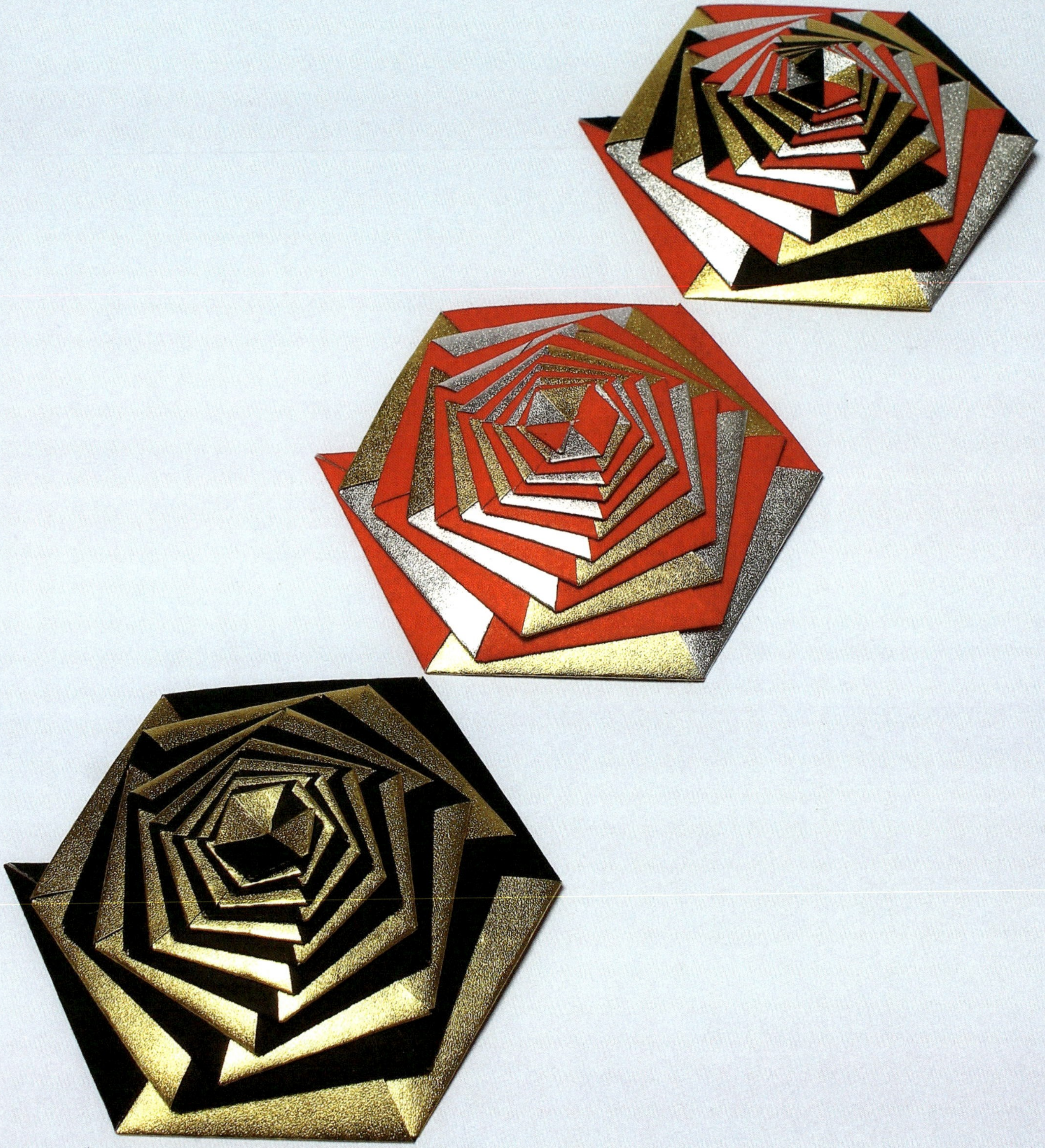

Double Hexagonal Curlicues

Before starting to fold, it's important to understand the form and geometry of this hexagonal spiral. A regular hexagon is composed of 60° and 120° angles. For the spiral hexagon some exterior angles are expanded and some are contracted slightly. The diagrams below show this.

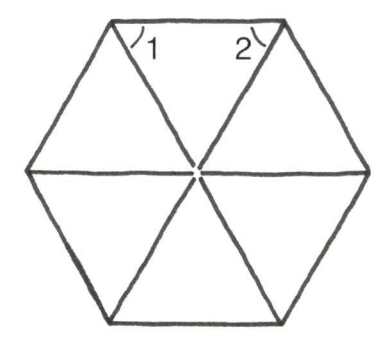

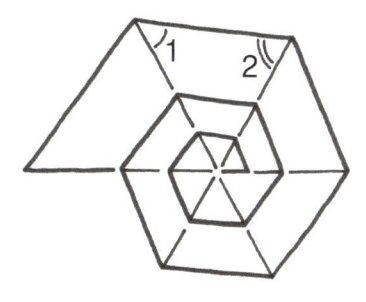

1 = 2 = 60°   1 < 60° < 2

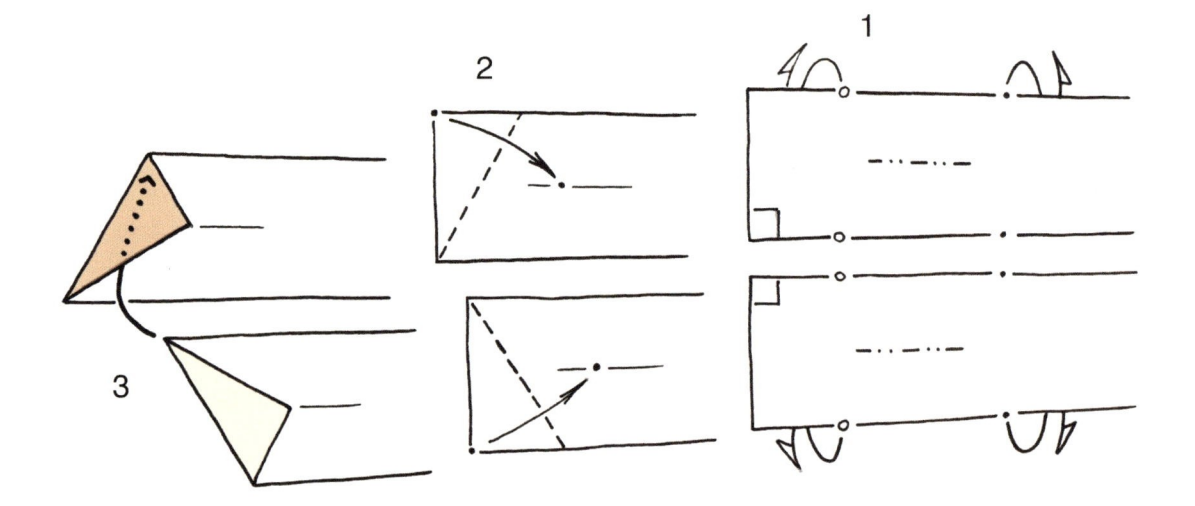

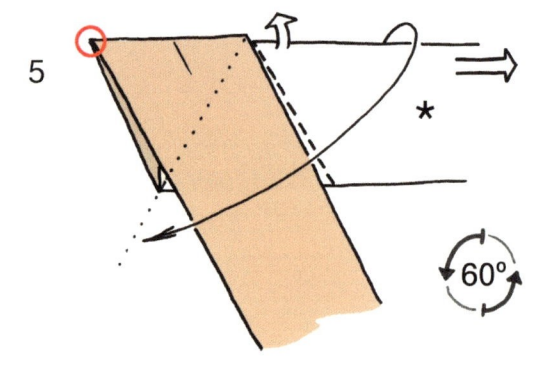

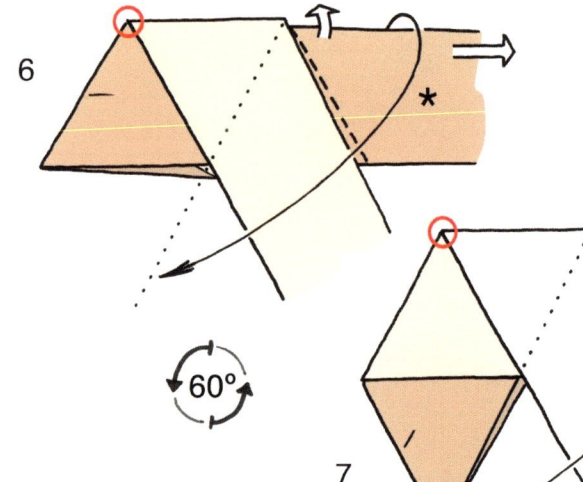

Double Hexagonal Curlicue

Prepare two tapering strips measuring, for example 70 x 3 x 1 cm. If you find it difficult to work at this scale, try 140 x 6 x 2 cm.

Step 4
The valley folding line lies along the short edge. The upper right-hand raw edge does not line up with the left-hand folded edge.

Steps 5 and 6 onwards
To eliminate the small "step" at the upper edge, pull the right hand strip slightly upwards and to the right. Hold the layers of the marked corner (O) tightly together to prevent any slippage during folding. Always fold the edge of the strip to touch the centre point: do not try to line up the new crease with the strip below.

Lift and release the lower strip (marked with *) from the edge below before moving to the next step. As you proceed, the corners of the hexagonal spiral will appear slightly twisted to the right and the diagonal "spokes" no longer form straight lines. See diagram 16 opposite.

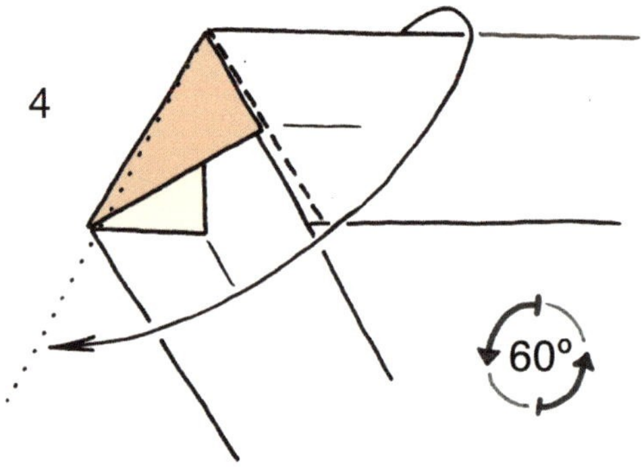

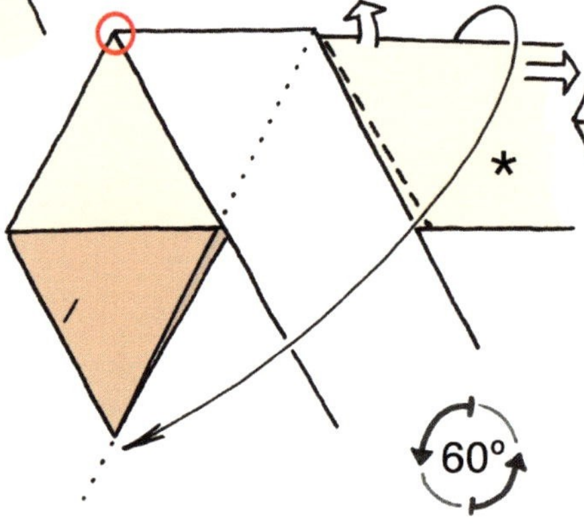

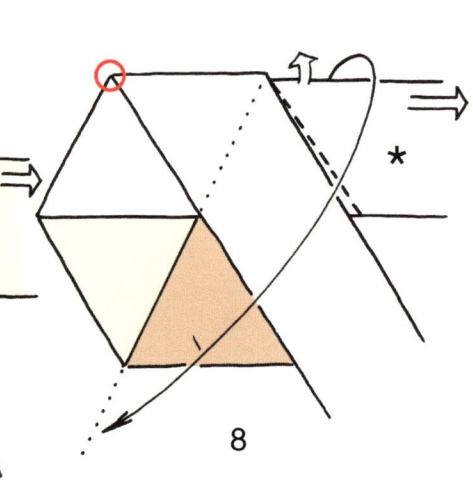

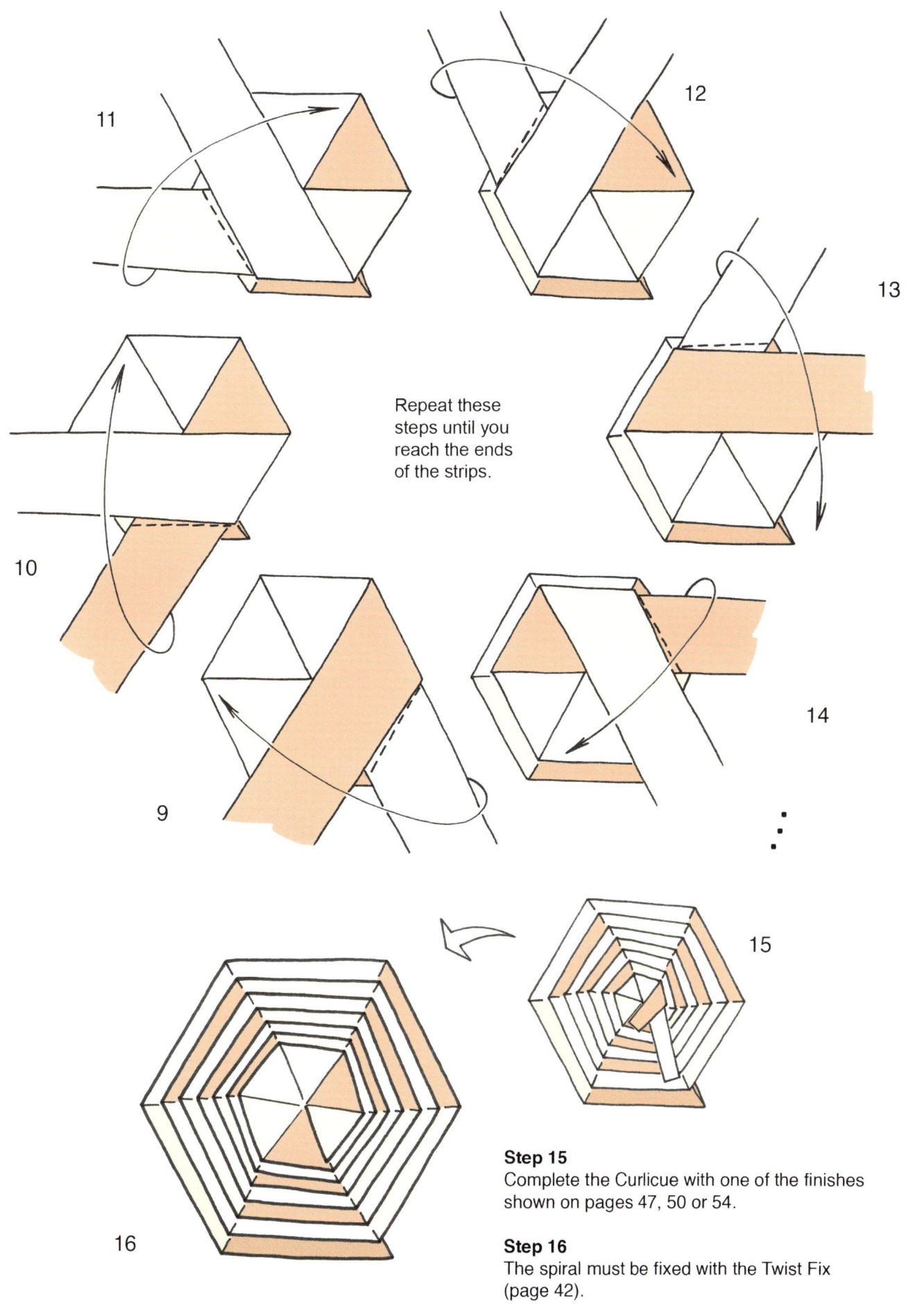

Repeat these steps until you reach the ends of the strips.

Step 15
Complete the Curlicue with one of the finishes shown on pages 47, 50 or 54.

Step 16
The spiral must be fixed with the Twist Fix (page 42).

41

Twist Fix for Hexagonal Curlicue

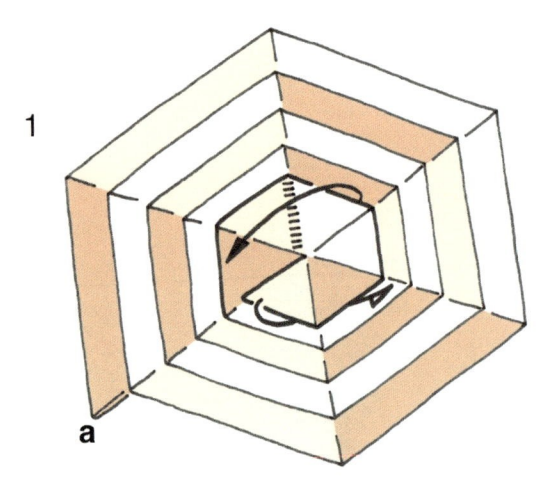

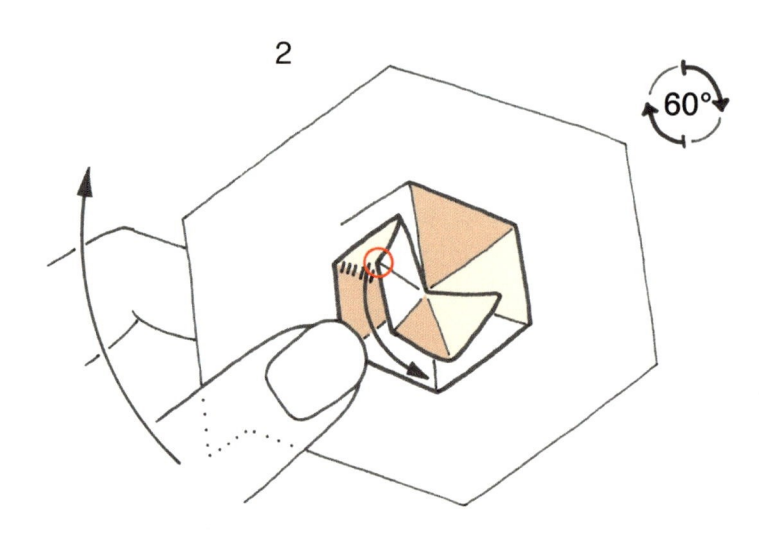

This procedure locks a free spiral, and must be made for all Curlicues which are folded by the Valley Fold method. For a full explanation of the twist procedure, see page 10. Remember that you should make gentle curves in the paper, not hard creases. No new folds are needed. In the diagrams, a valley curve symbol IIIII indicates this.

NB: For clarity, not all layers are shown in diagrams 2–8.

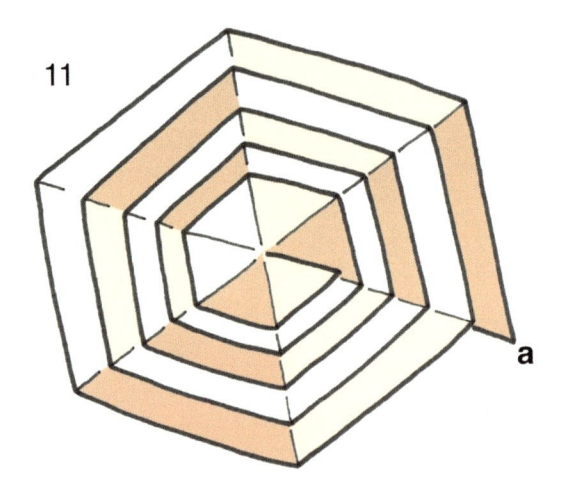

Step 1
Making a soft valley fold, lift the first four triangular sections at the small end of the spiral and swing the corner underneath and to the right.

Step 2
All the layers which have not yet been locked are held together flat by the left hand. The left hand moves the model clockwise.
The repositioned section is held by the right hand at the point indicated by the red circle. The right hand rotates this section anti-clockwise.

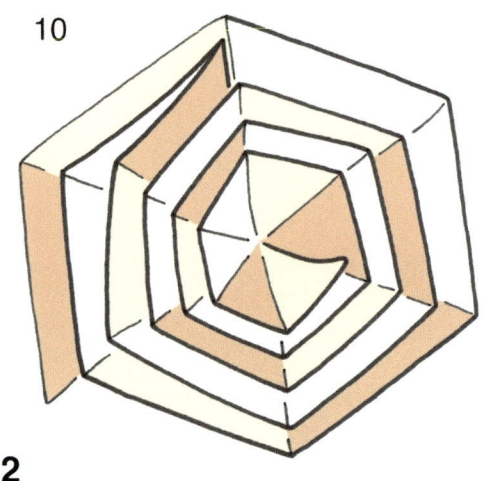

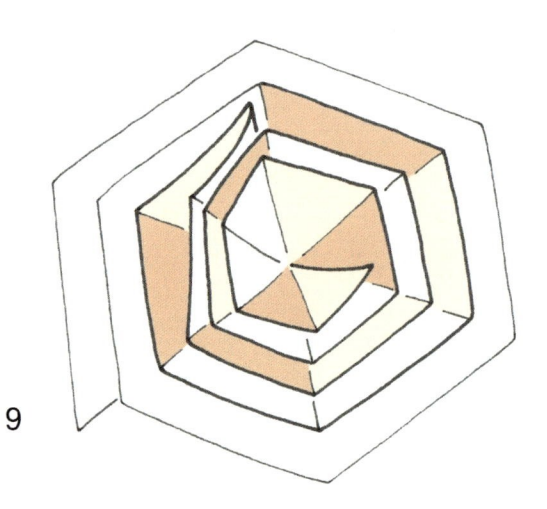

42

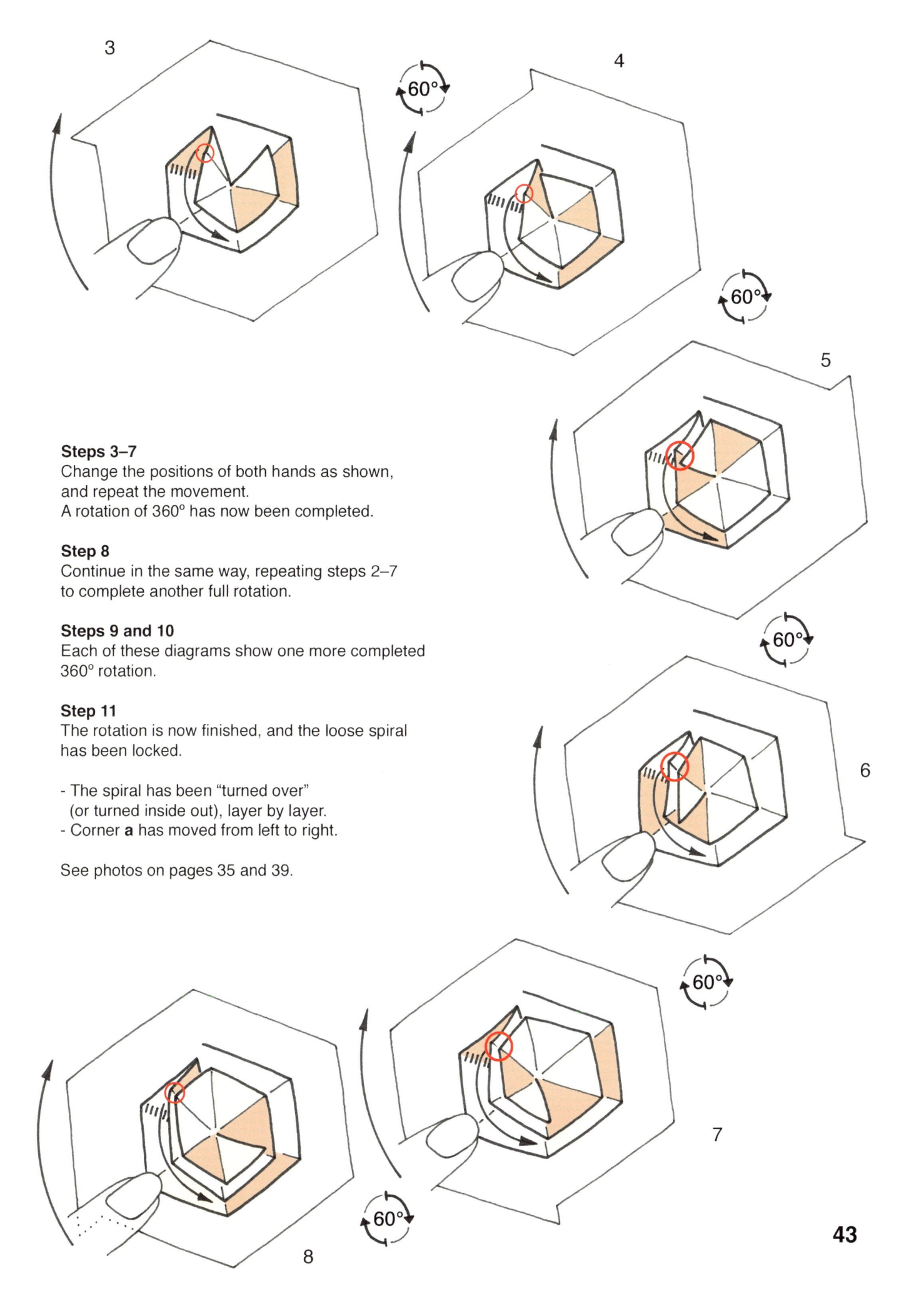

Steps 3–7
Change the positions of both hands as shown, and repeat the movement.
A rotation of 360° has now been completed.

Step 8
Continue in the same way, repeating steps 2–7 to complete another full rotation.

Steps 9 and 10
Each of these diagrams show one more completed 360° rotation.

Step 11
The rotation is now finished, and the loose spiral has been locked.

- The spiral has been "turned over" (or turned inside out), layer by layer.
- Corner **a** has moved from left to right.

See photos on pages 35 and 39.

43

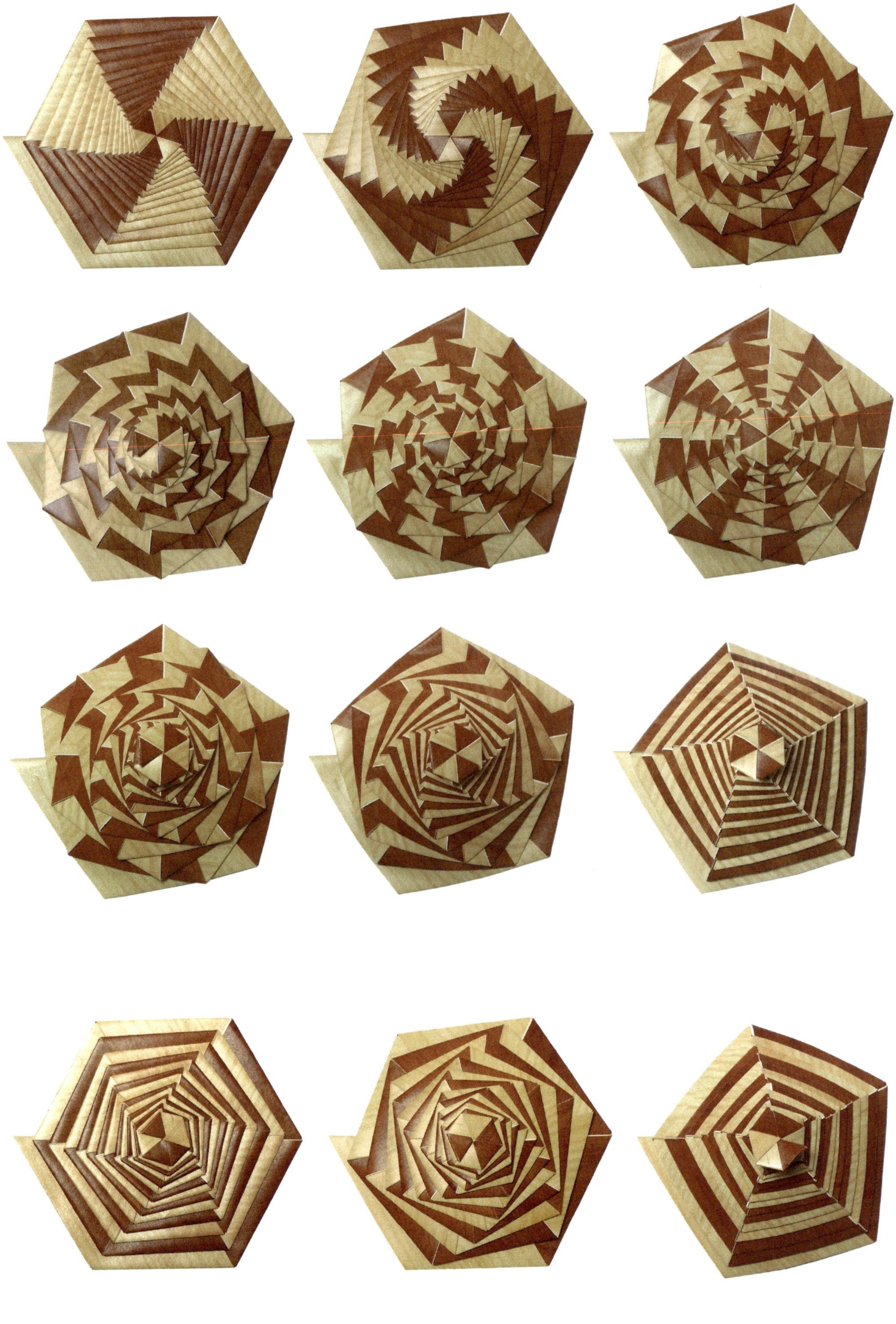

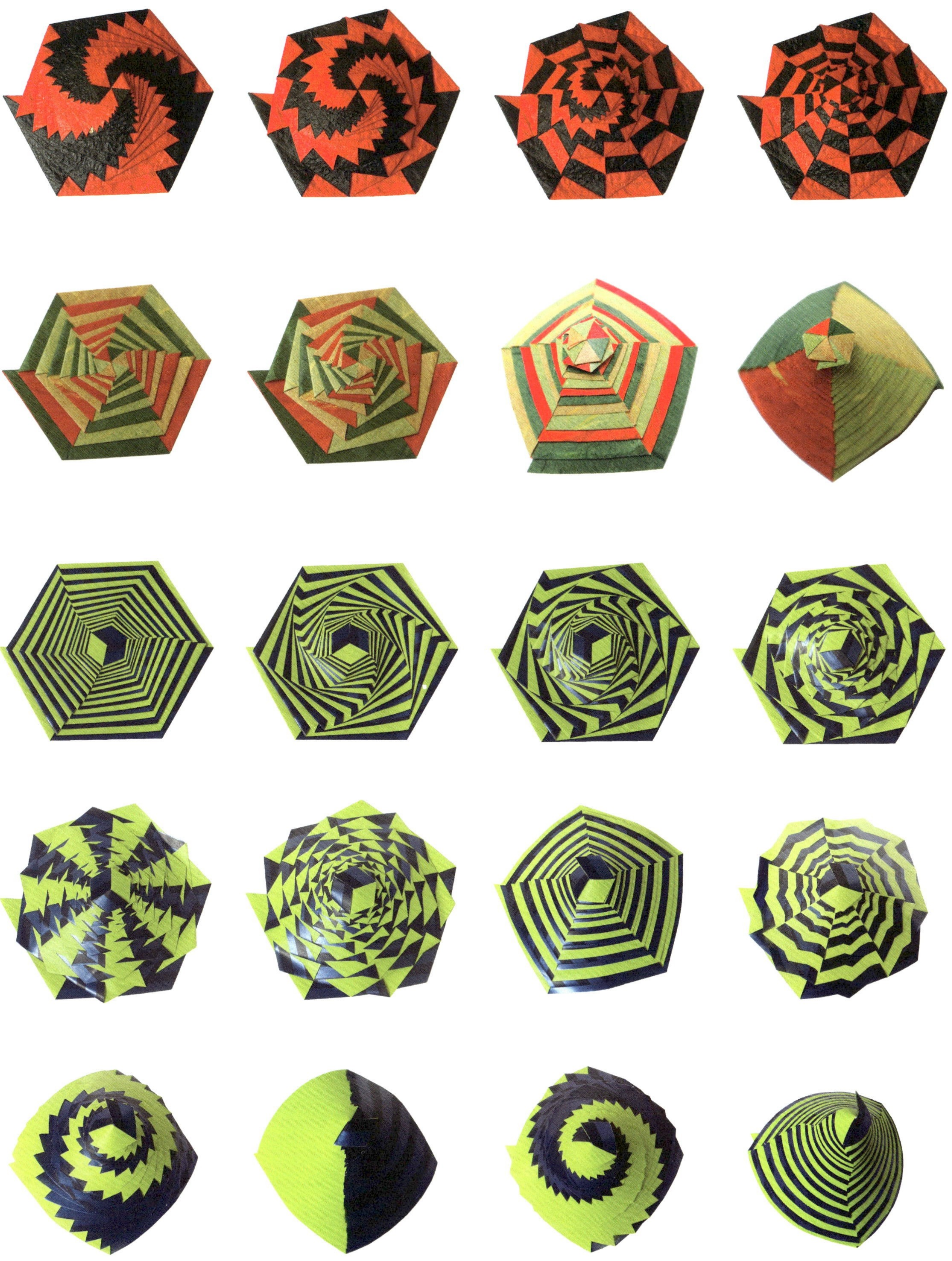

Securing the two strips

While experimenting with different folding materials, I realised that it was necessary to improve the locking of the ends of the Double Hexagonal Curlicue, so I developed some variations of the lock:

- *The Simple Connection* is the basic method.
- *The Single Lock* is a secure method for connecting paper strips.
- *The Double Lock* is a very secure lock, good for both plastic and paper.

Here are the starting and finishing procedures for Valley and Mountain Fold methods. These work for both parallel and tapering strips.

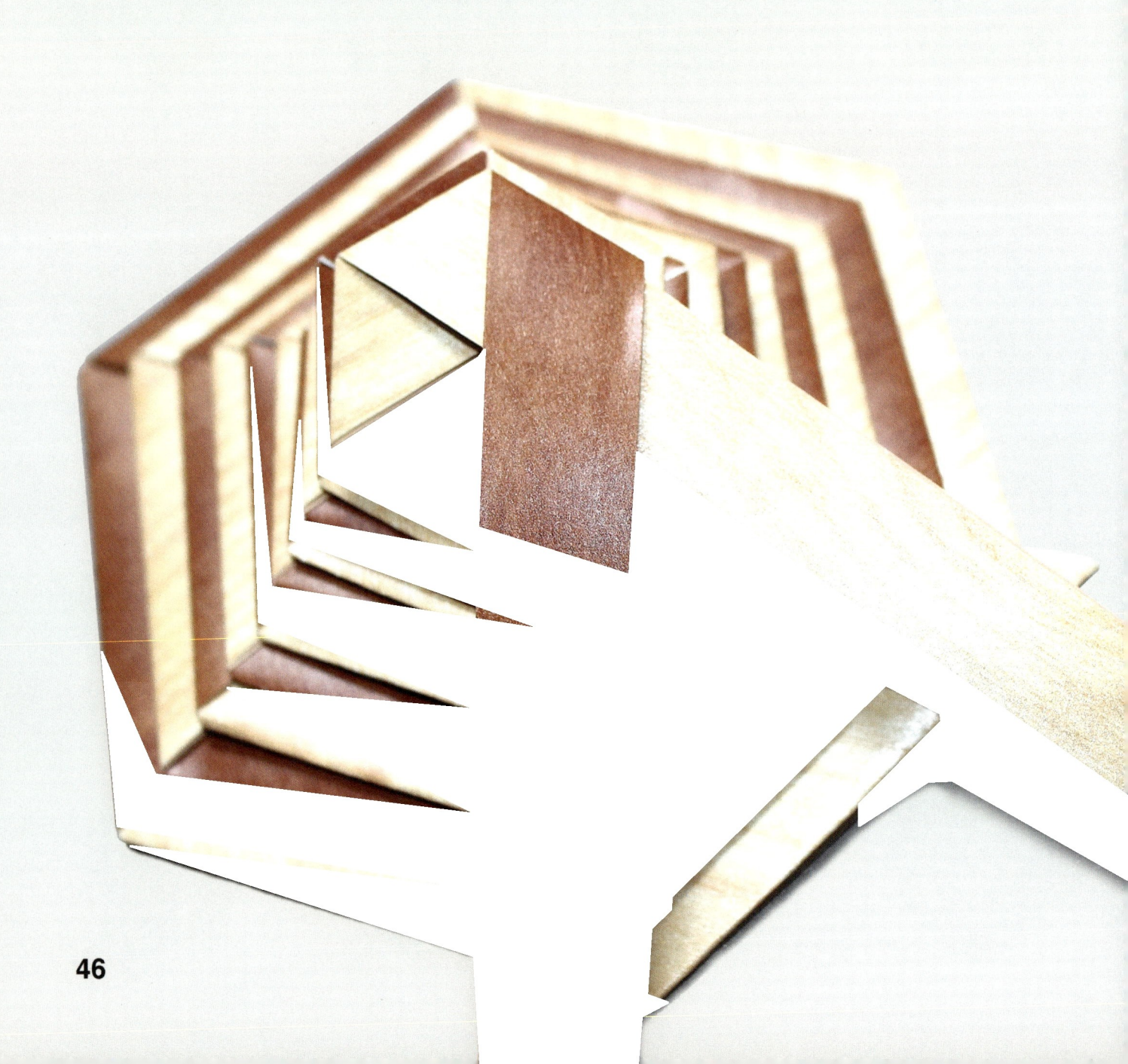

Simple Connection Start

Start for Valley and Mountain Fold methods.

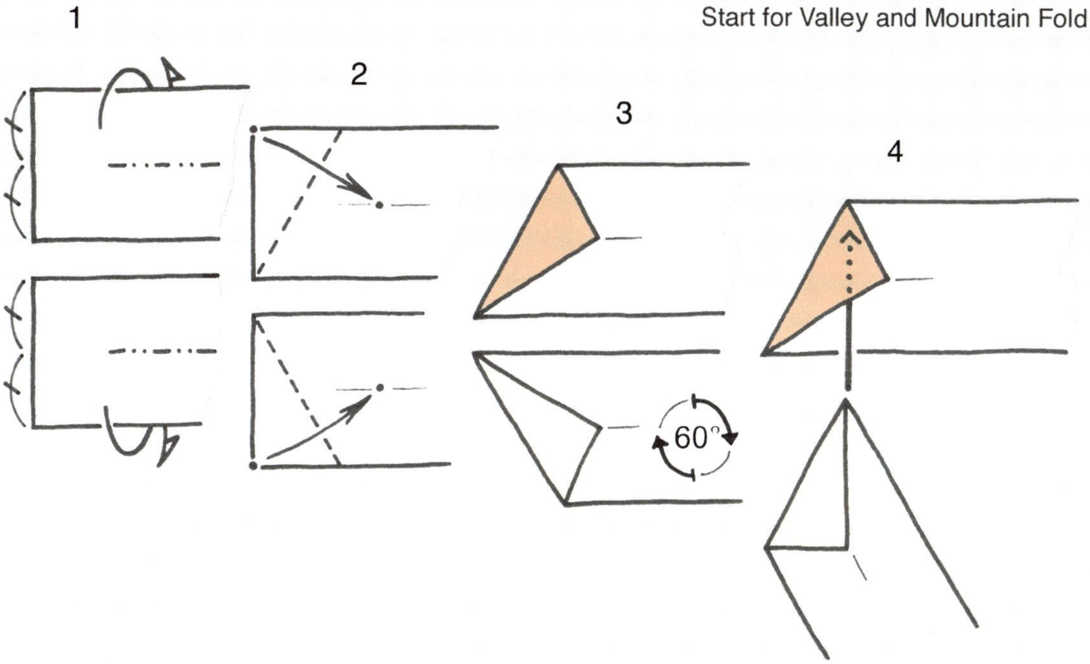

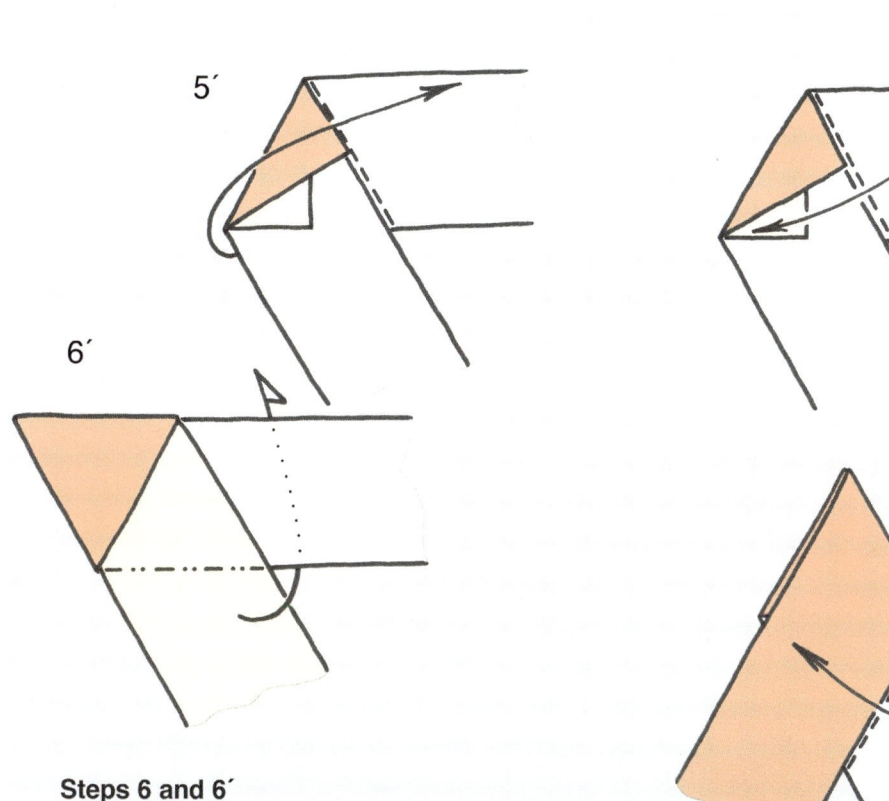

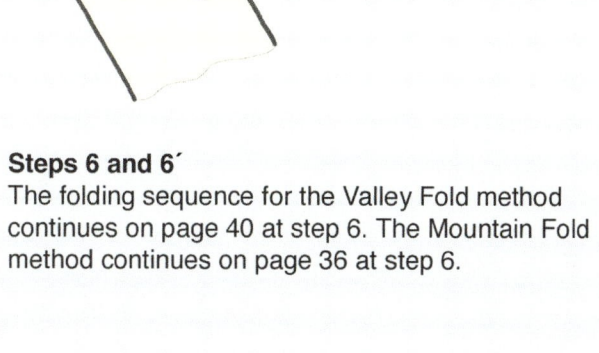

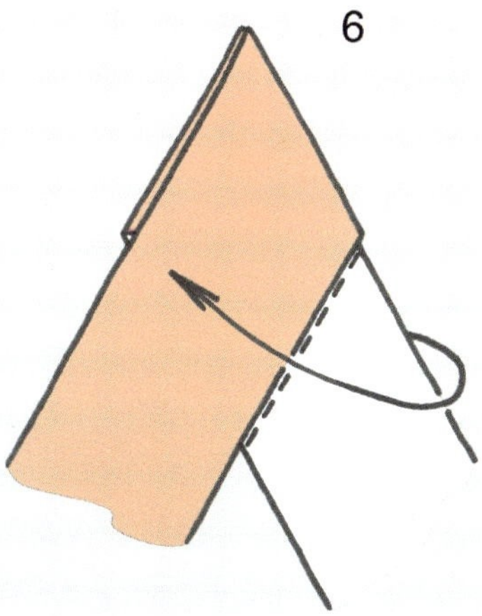

Steps 6 and 6´
The folding sequence for the Valley Fold method continues on page 40 at step 6. The Mountain Fold method continues on page 36 at step 6.

47

Simple Connection Finishes

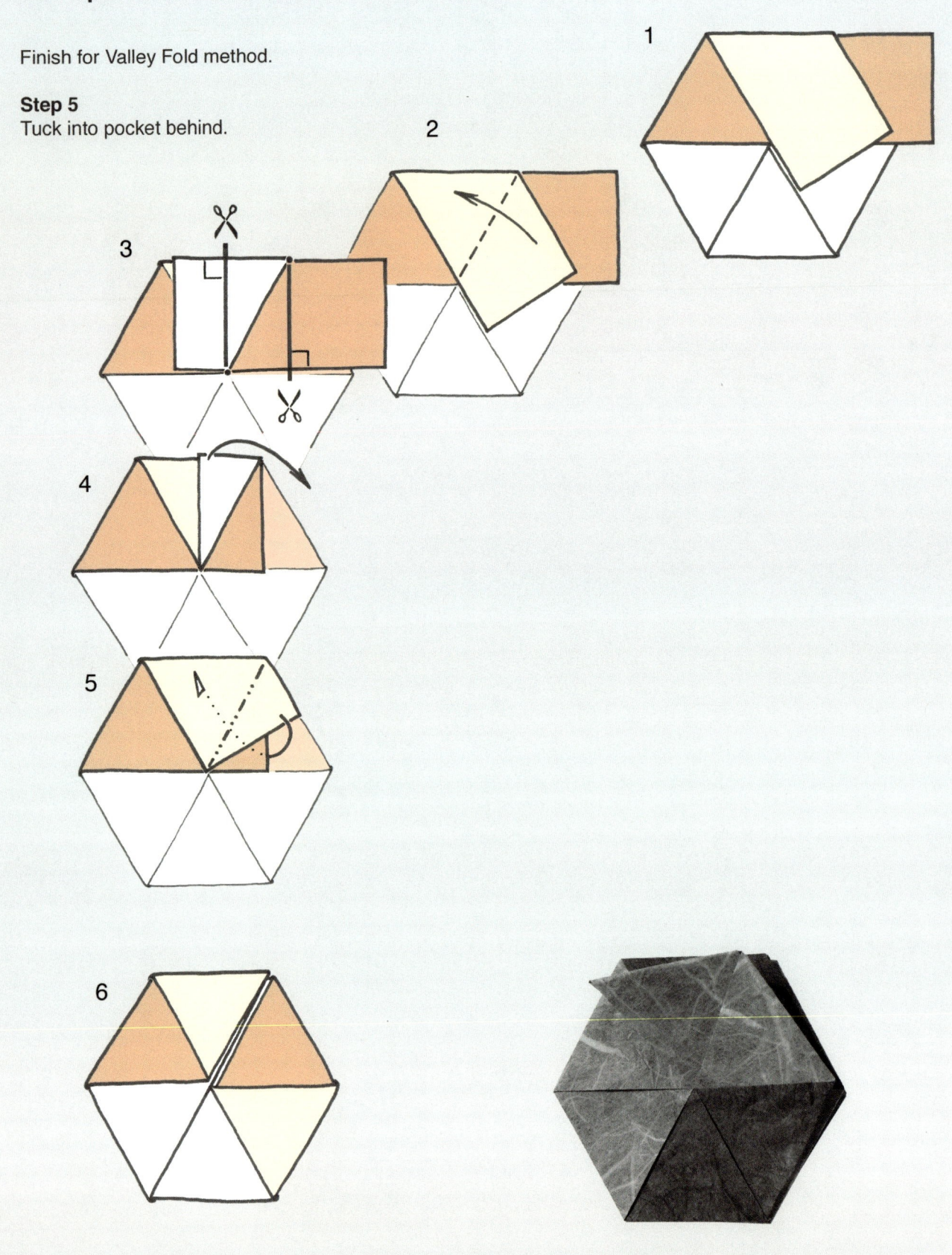

Finish for Valley Fold method.

Step 5
Tuck into pocket behind.

48

Finish for Mountain Fold method.

1

2

3

4

5

6

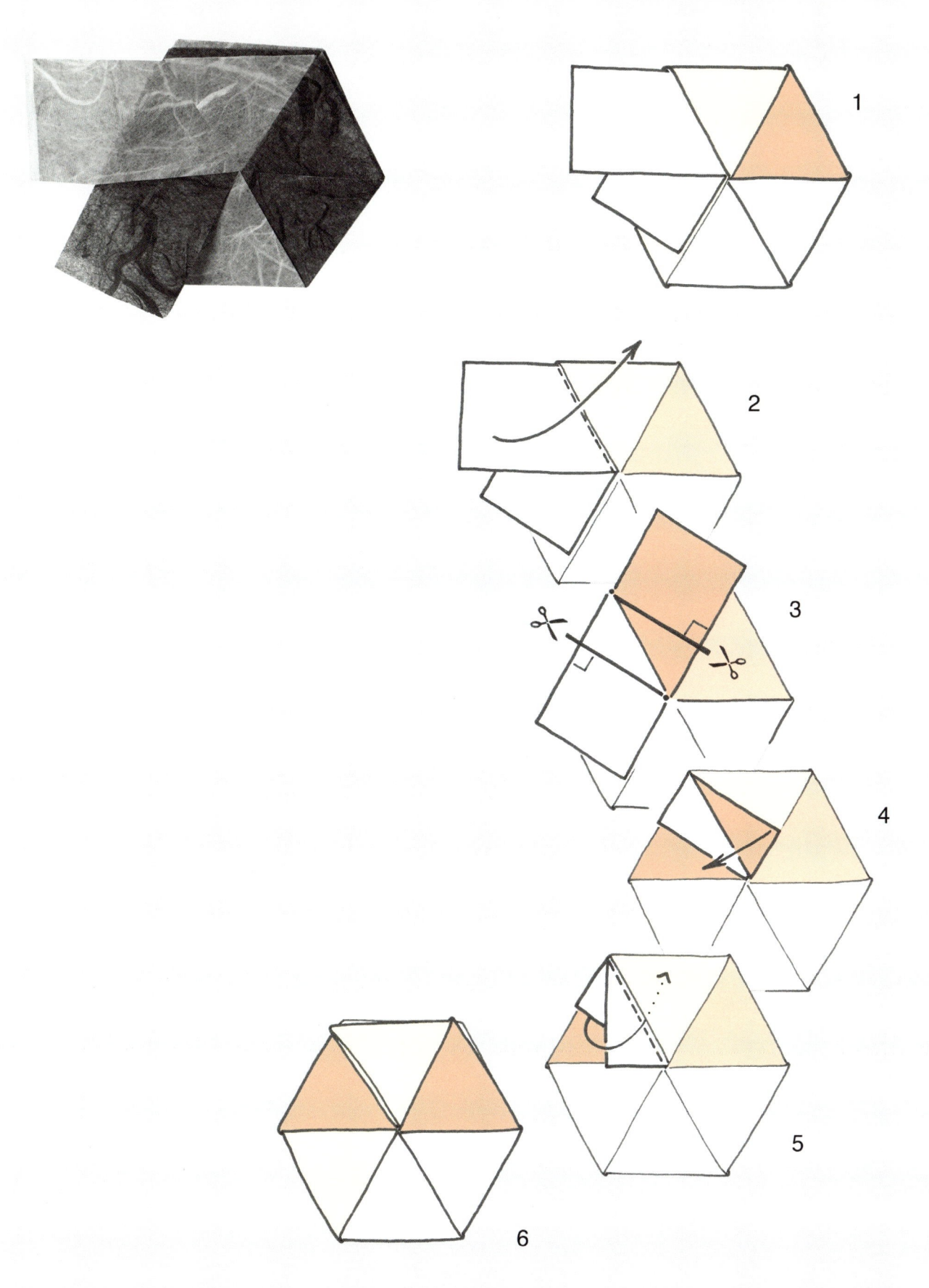

Single Lock Start

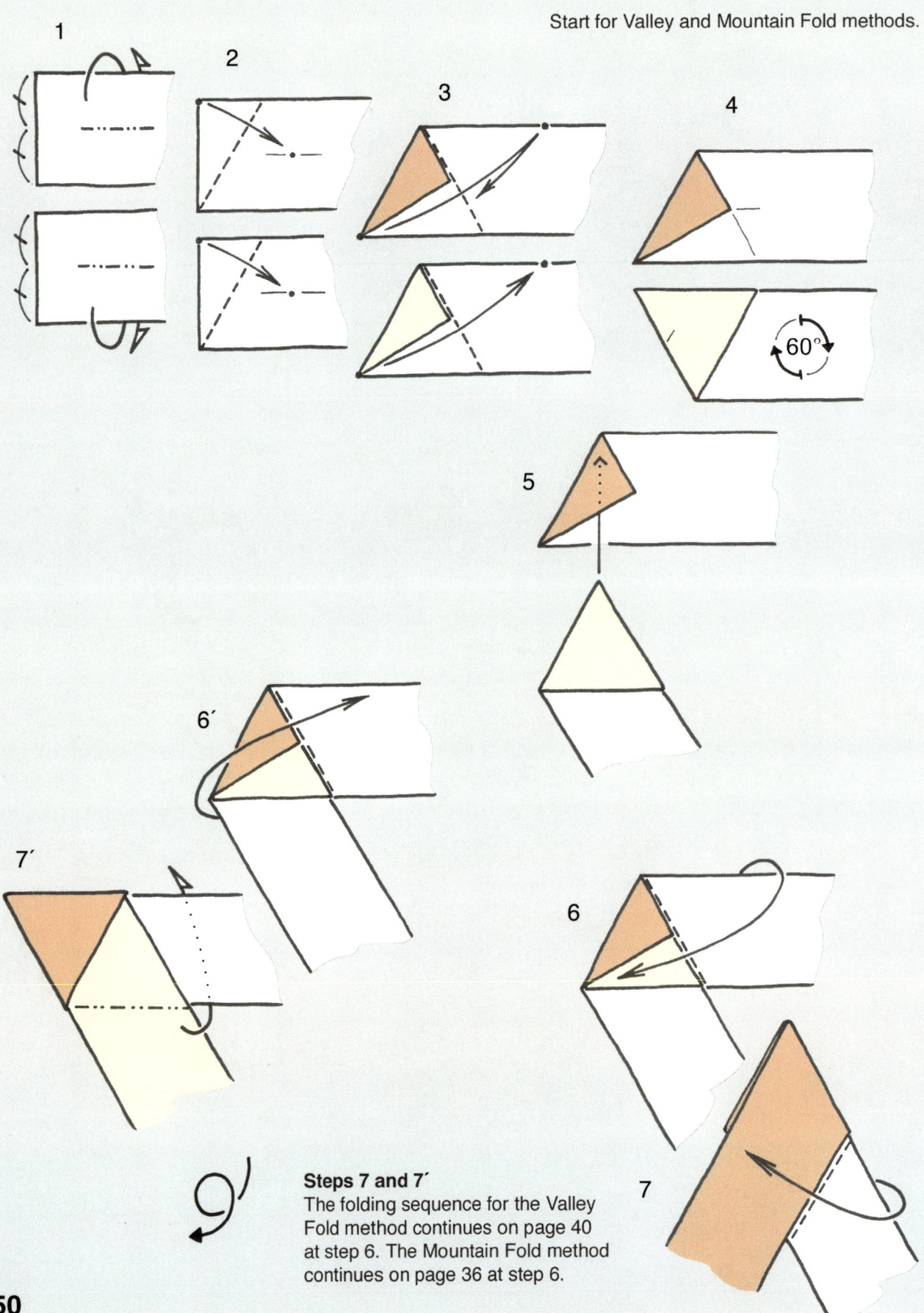

Start for Valley and Mountain Fold methods.

Steps 7 and 7´
The folding sequence for the Valley Fold method continues on page 40 at step 6. The Mountain Fold method continues on page 36 at step 6.

50

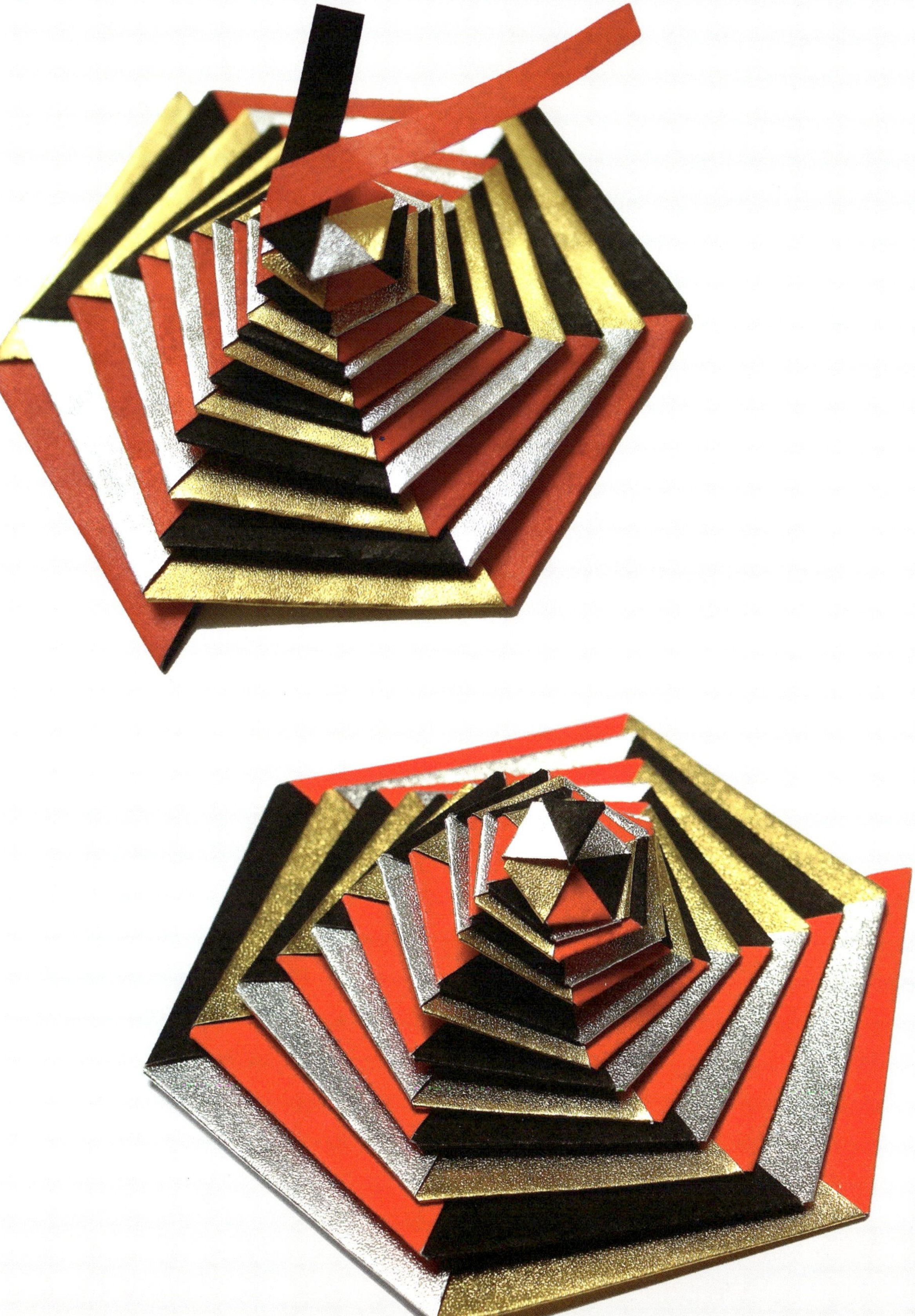

Single Lock Finishes

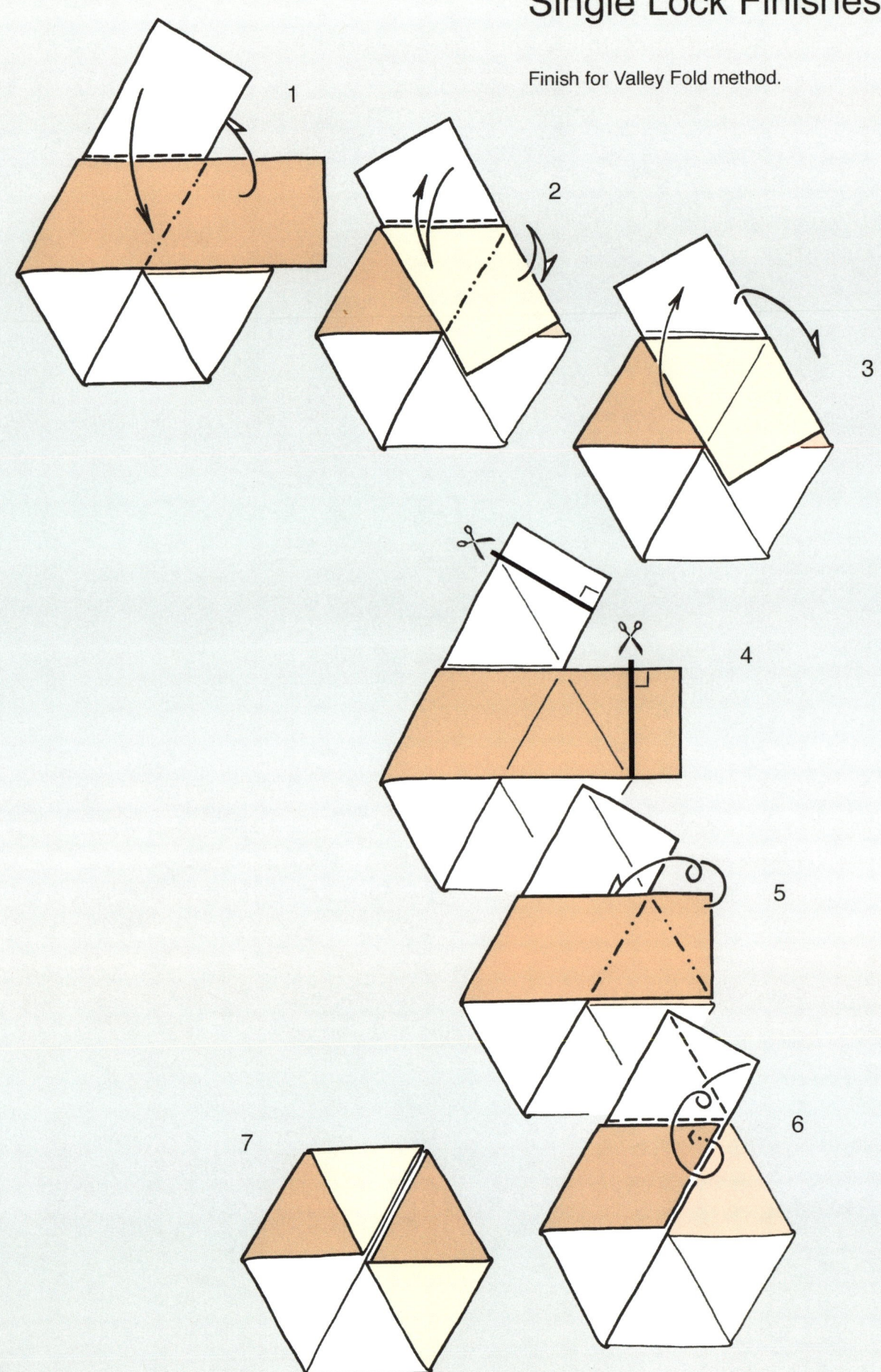

Finish for Valley Fold method.

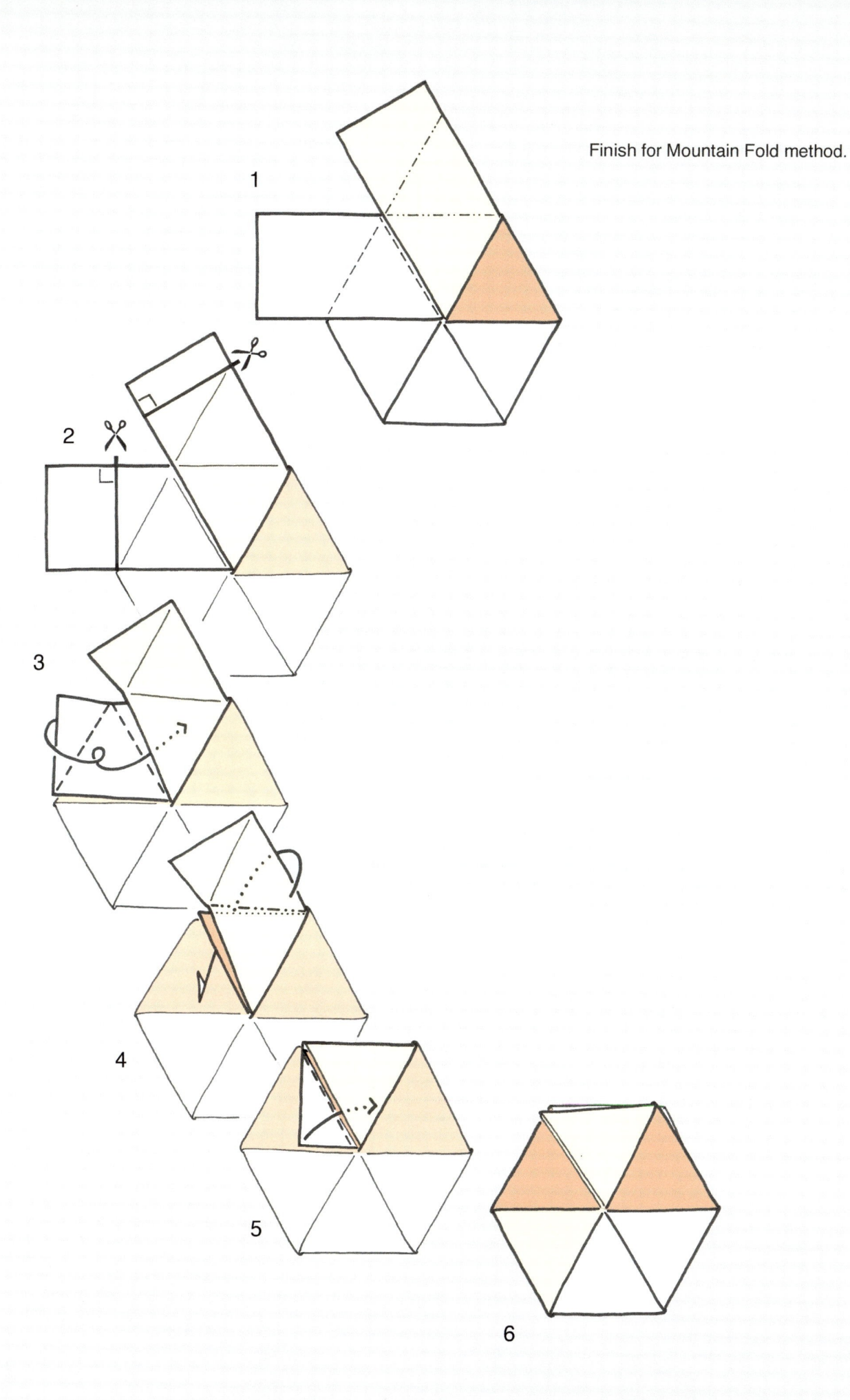

Finish for Mountain Fold method.

1

2

3

4

5

6

53

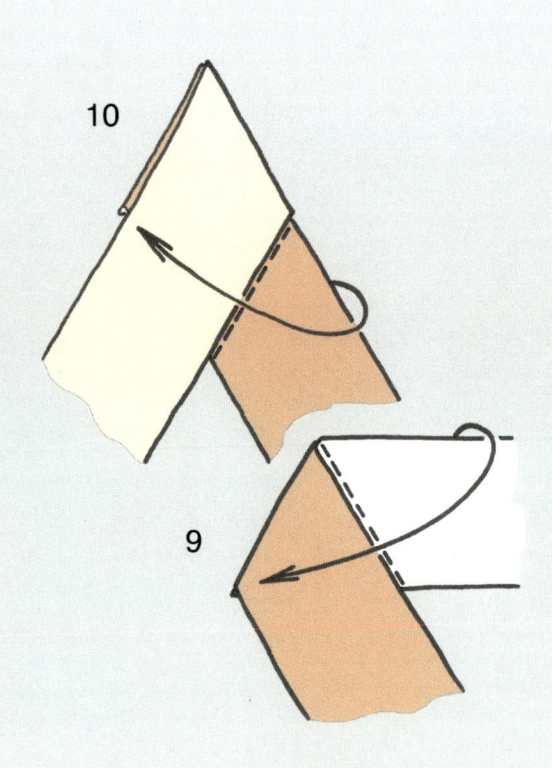

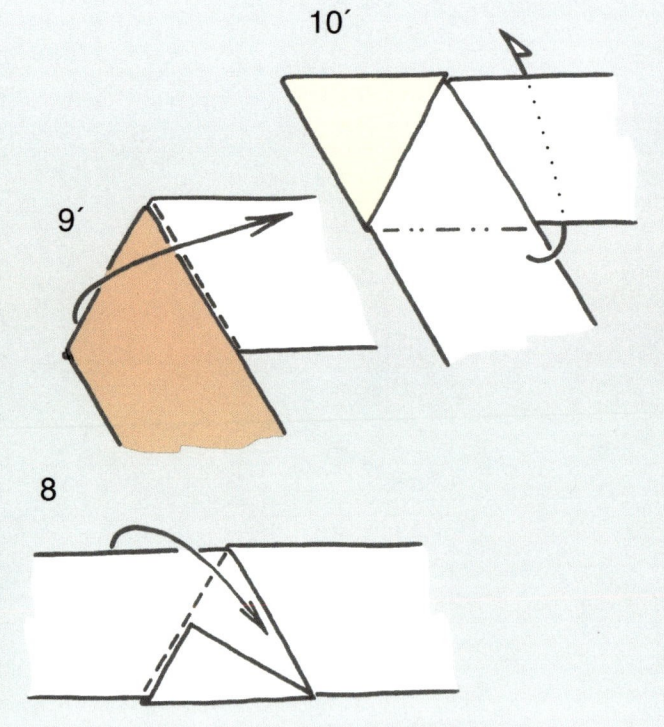

Double Lock Start

Start for Valley and Mountain Fold methods.

Step 4
Repeat steps 1, 2 and 3 on a second strip.

Step 10
The folding sequence for the Valley Fold method continues on page 40 at step 6.

Step 10´
For the Mountain Fold method continue on page 36 at step 6.

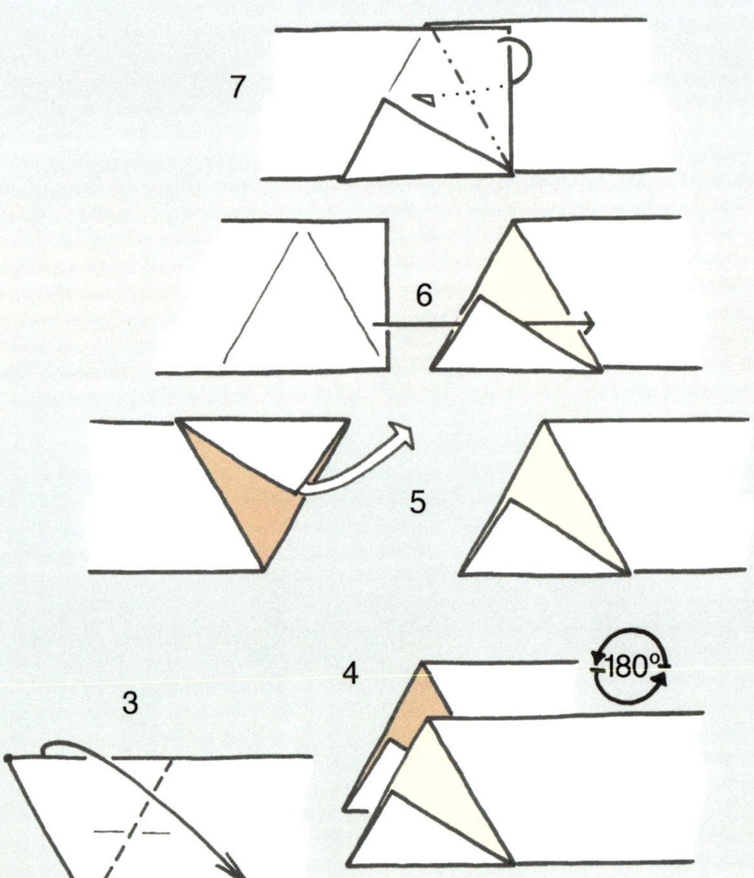

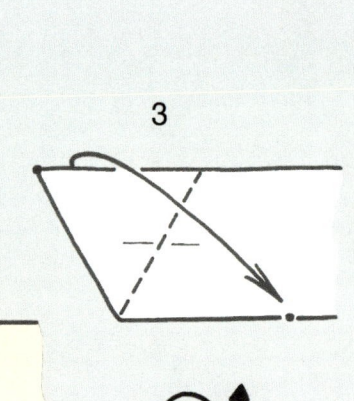

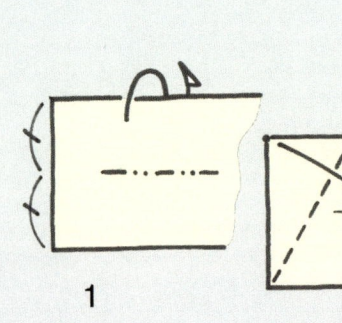

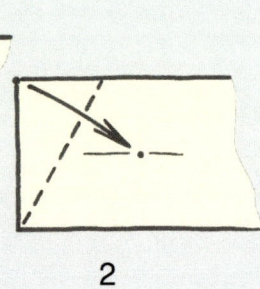

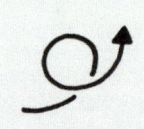

54

Double Lock Finish

Finish for Valley Fold method.

Note, finish for Mountain Fold method not shown.

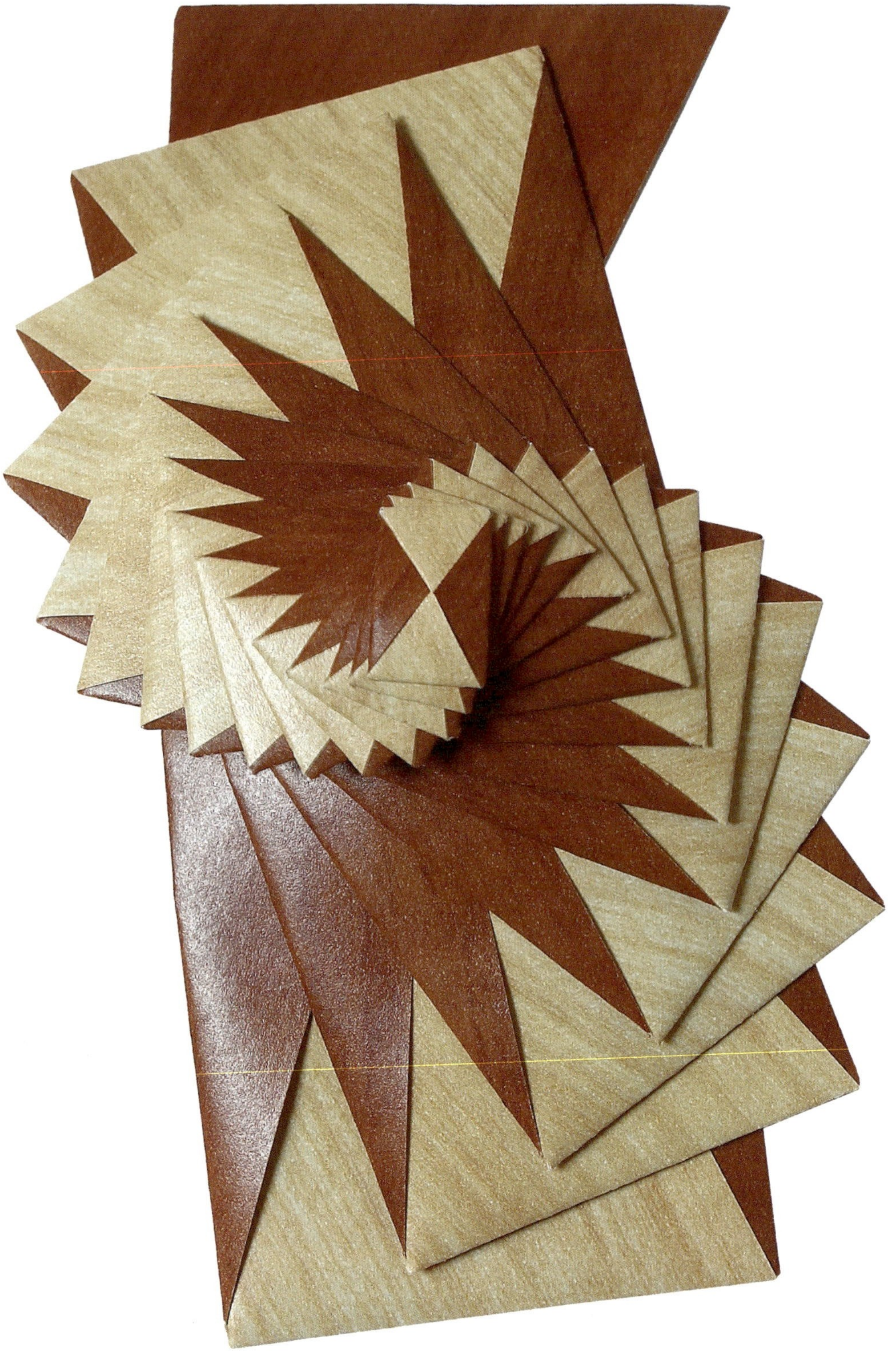

4

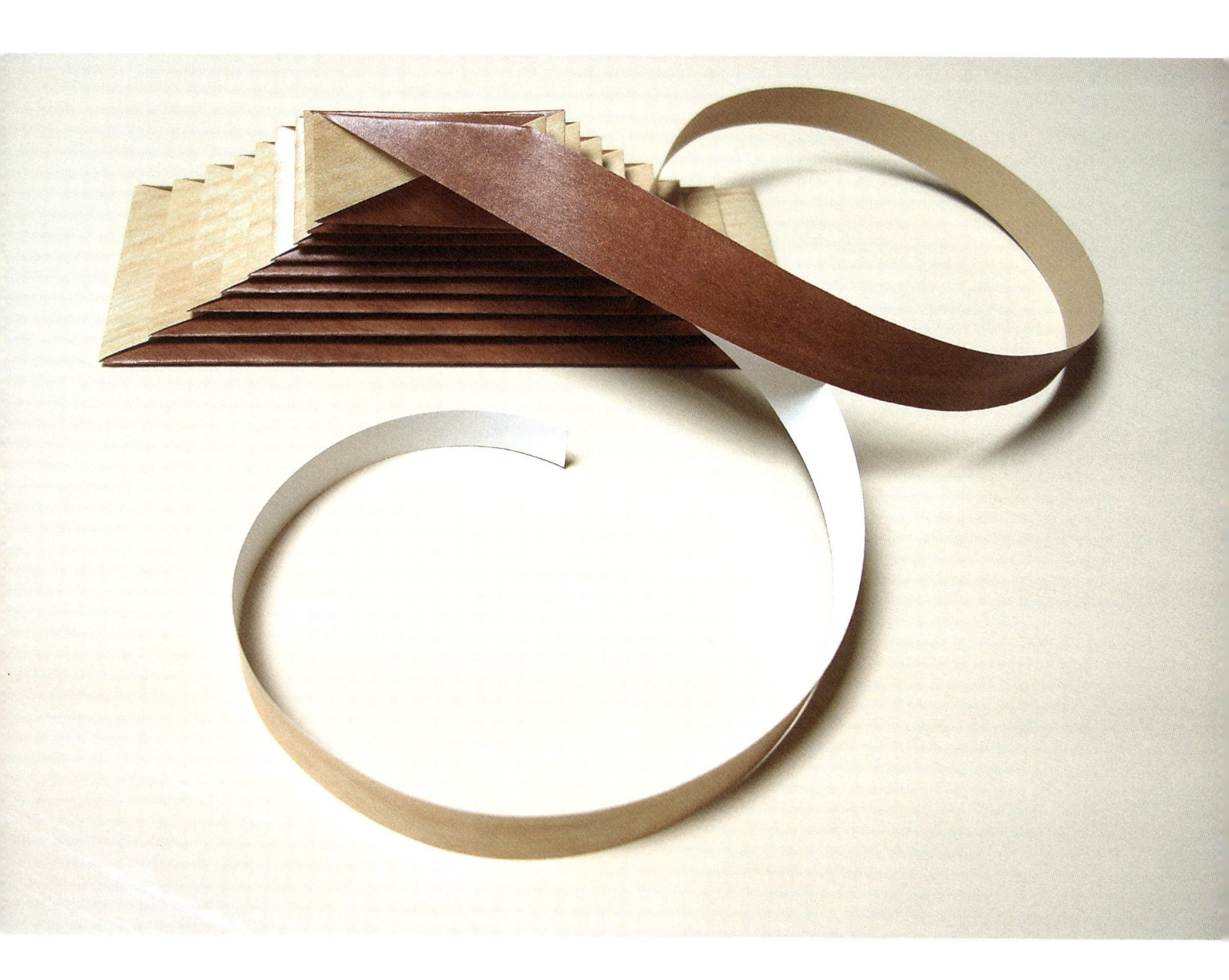

Rectangular Curlicues

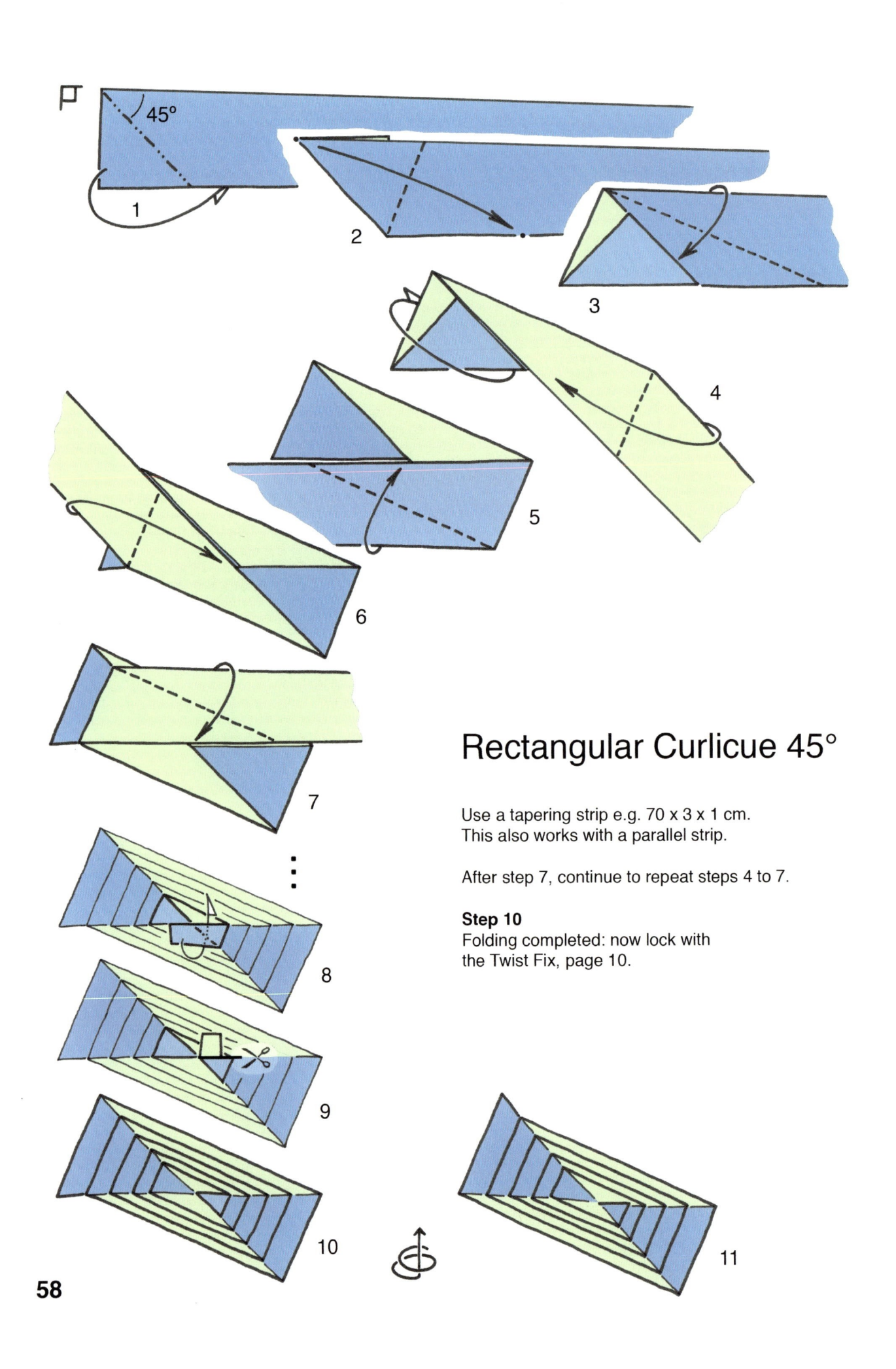

Rectangular Curlicue 45°

Use a tapering strip e.g. 70 x 3 x 1 cm.
This also works with a parallel strip.

After step 7, continue to repeat steps 4 to 7.

Step 10
Folding completed: now lock with the Twist Fix, page 10.

Prism Rectangular Curlicue 60°

Try with a very long parallel strip for best results. Also works with a tapering strip.

After step 9, continue to repeat steps 6 to 9.

Step 11
Folding completed: now lock with the Twist Fix, page 10.

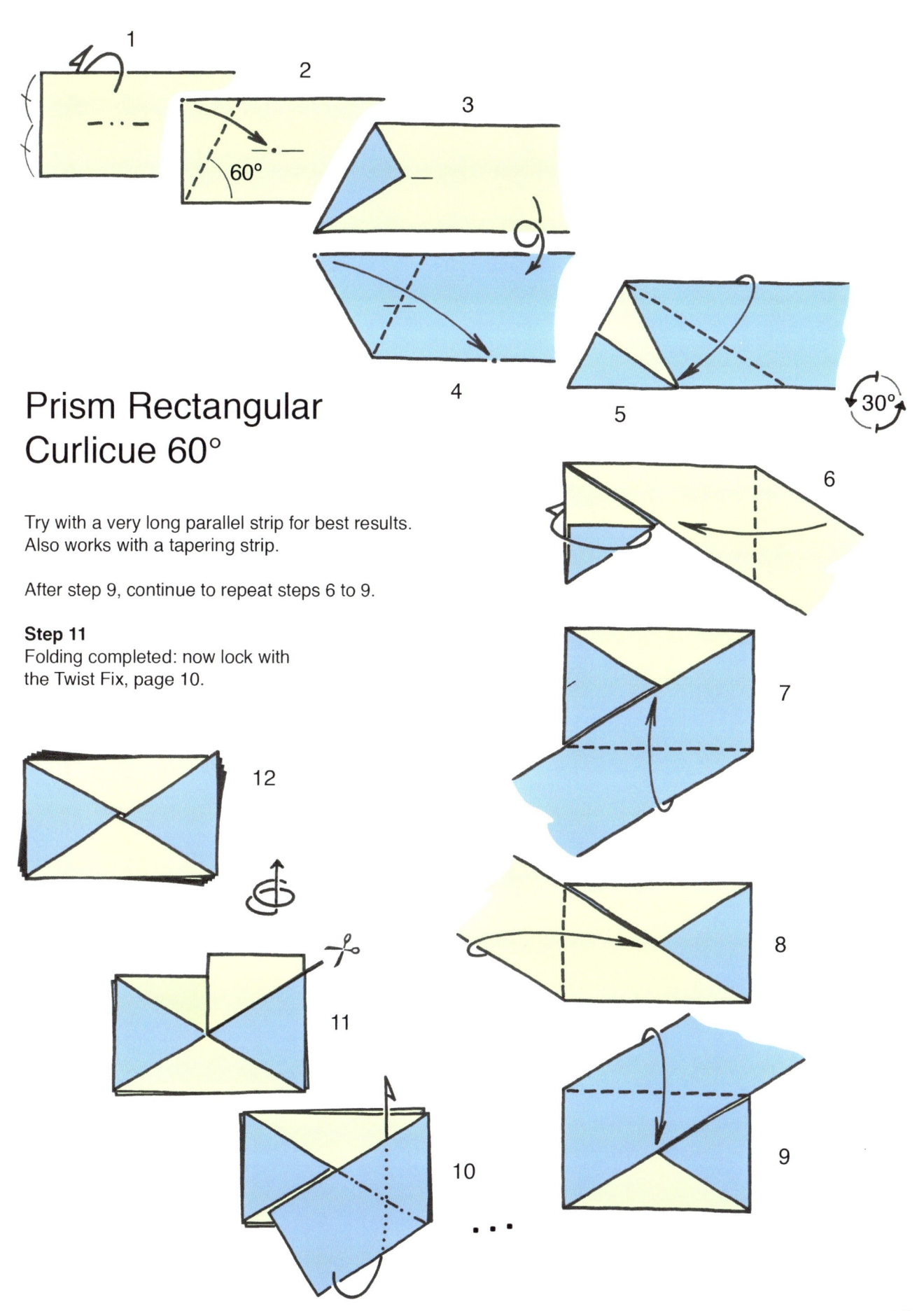

59

Double Rectangular Curlicue 45°

Use two tapering strips e.g. 70 x 3 x 1 cm. This also works with parallel strips.

Step 9
As with the Double Square Curlicue, page 23, use a repetitive folding method: mountain, valley, rotate; mountain, valley, rotate; etc. until the ends of the strips.

Step 14
Folding completed: now lock with the Twist Fix, page 10.

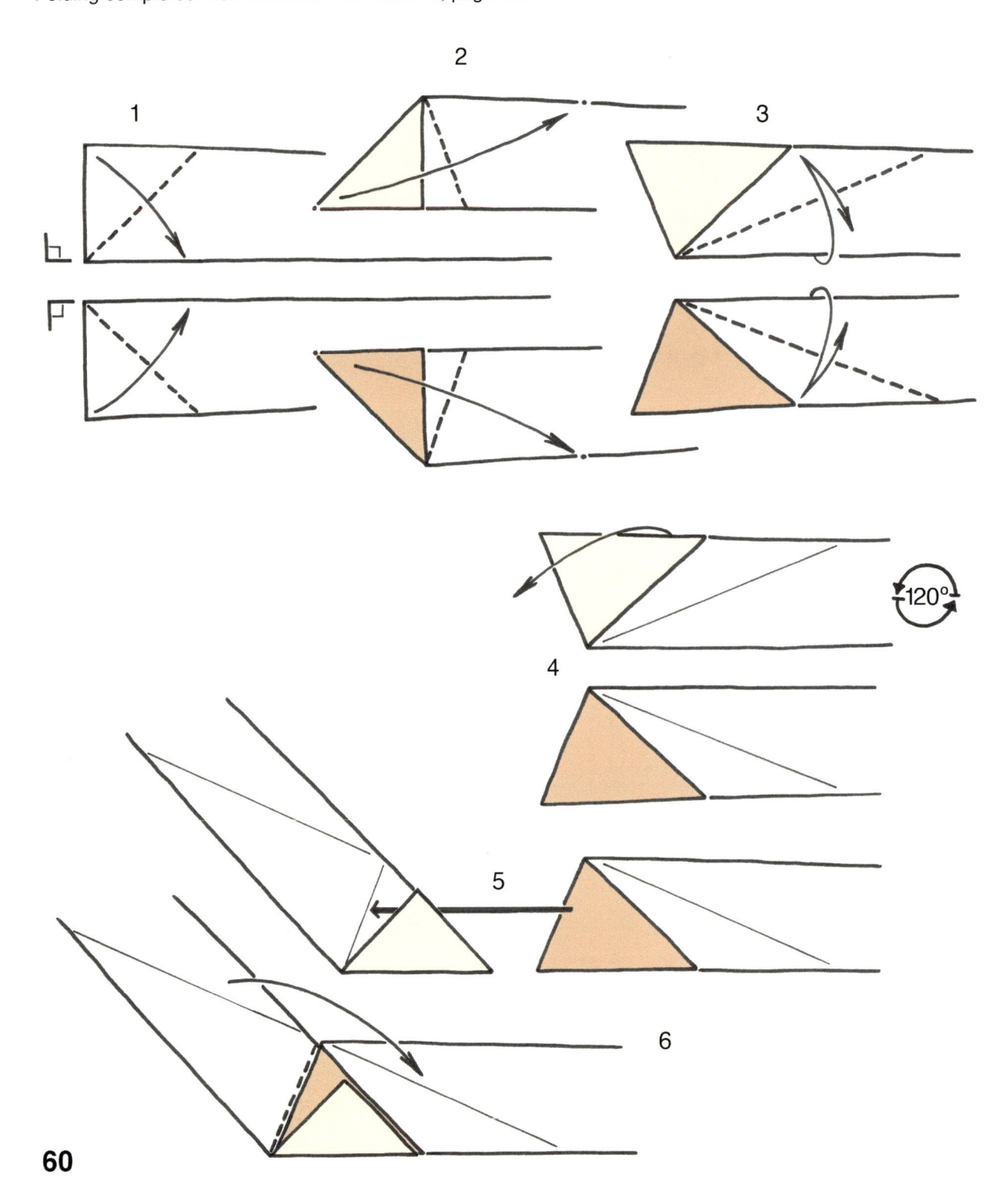

60

61

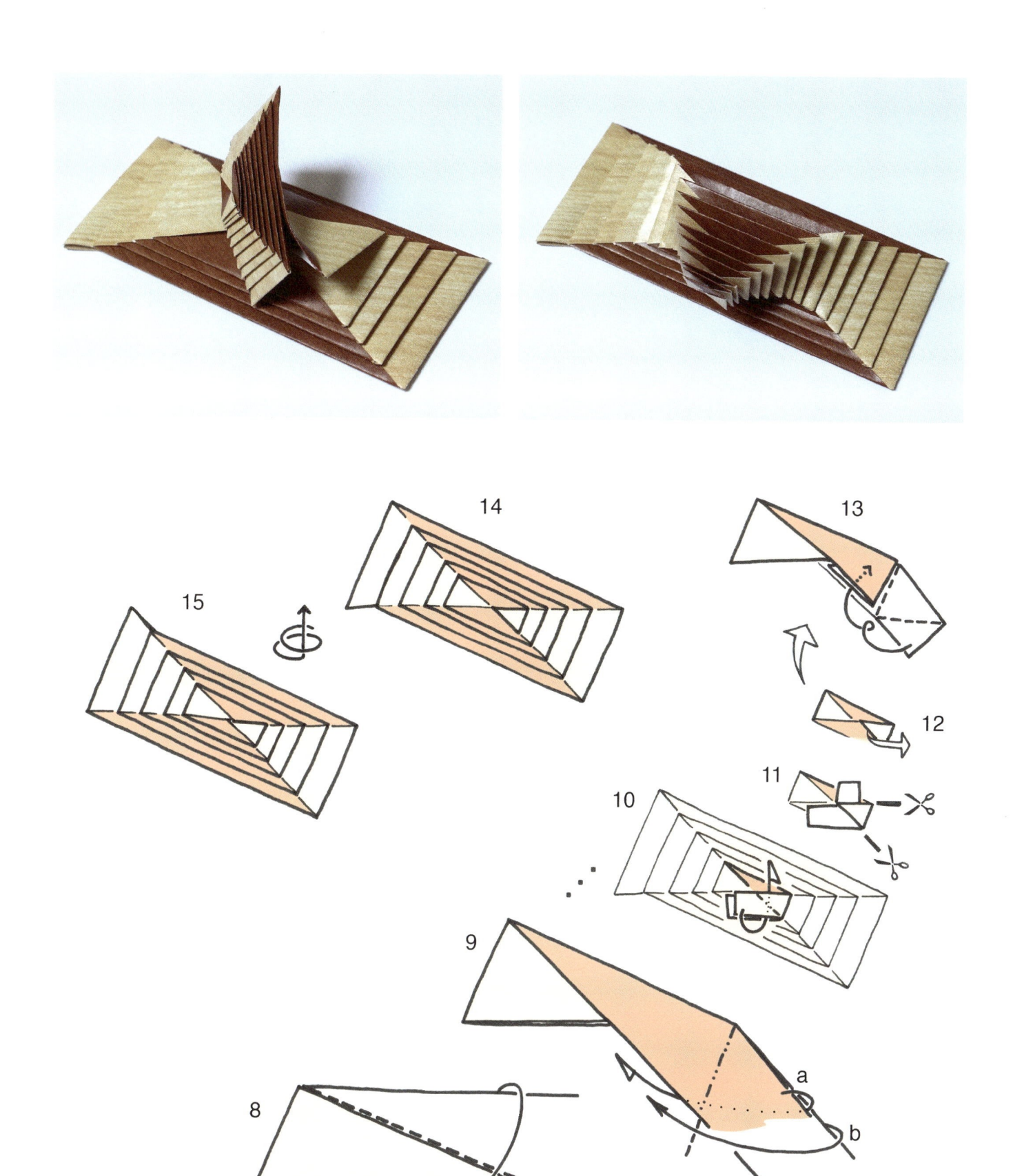

Double Prism Rectangular Curlicue 45°

Made from a single parallel strip folded in half. Also works with a tapering strip.

Step 4
Unfold completely.

Step 5
Reform, pushing the V-shaped area between the layers (reverse fold).

Step 8
As with the Double Prism Square Curlicue, page 27, use a repetitive folding method: mountain, valley, rotate; mountain, valley, rotate; etc. until the ends of the strips. Finish off as shown on page 61 starting at step 10.

Folding completed: now lock with the Twist Fix, page 10.

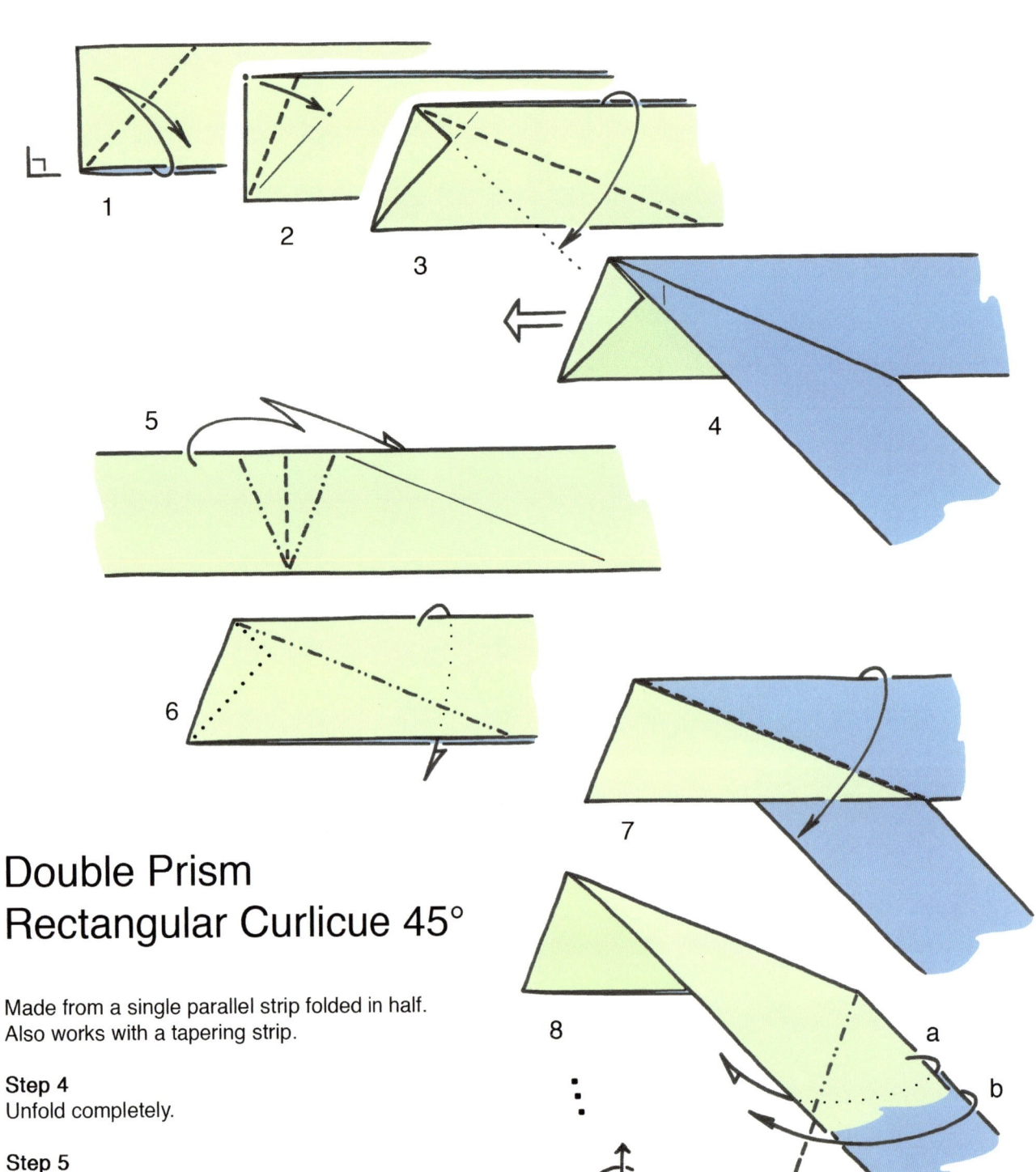

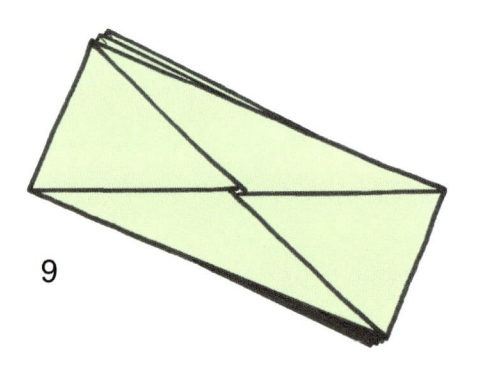

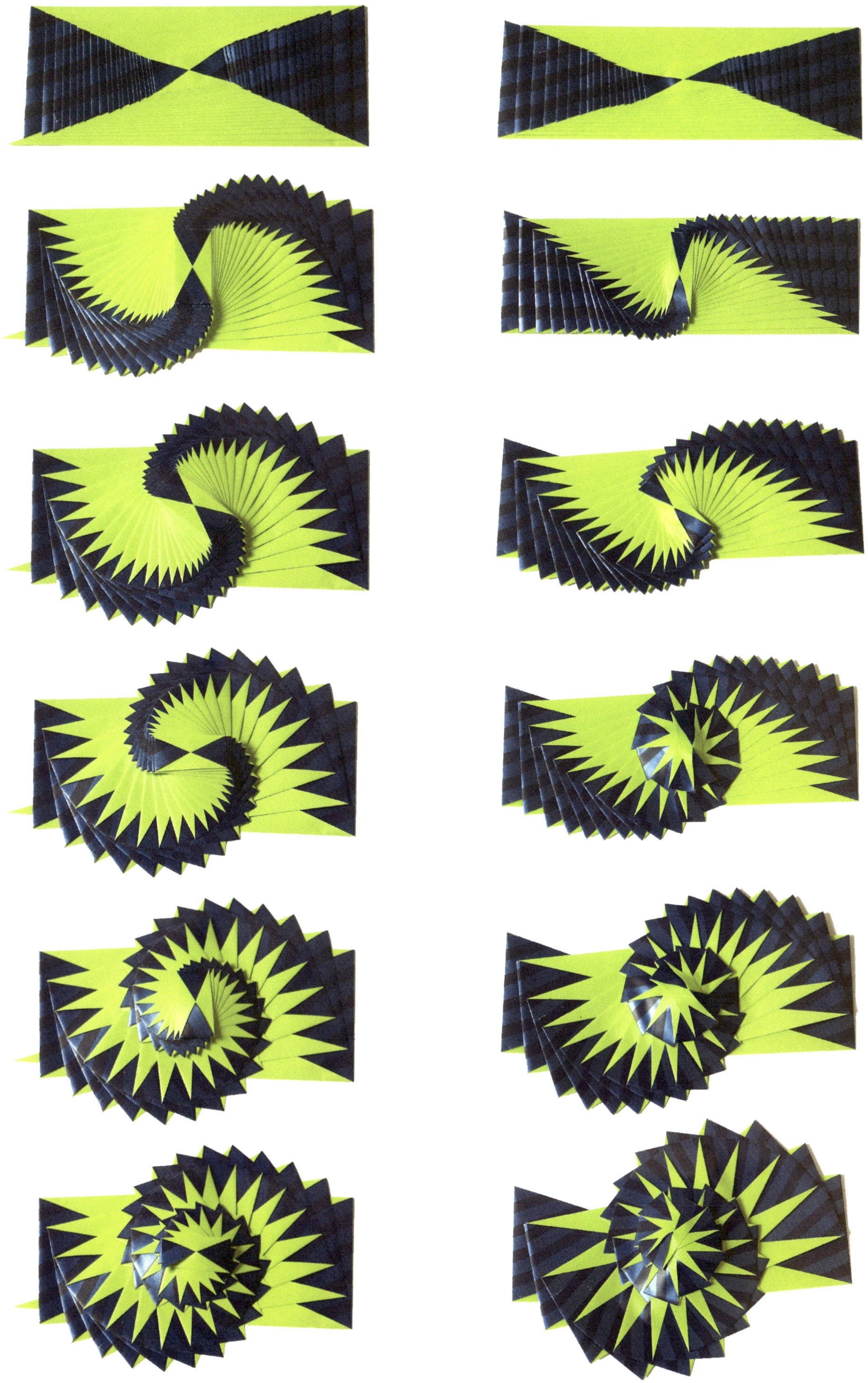

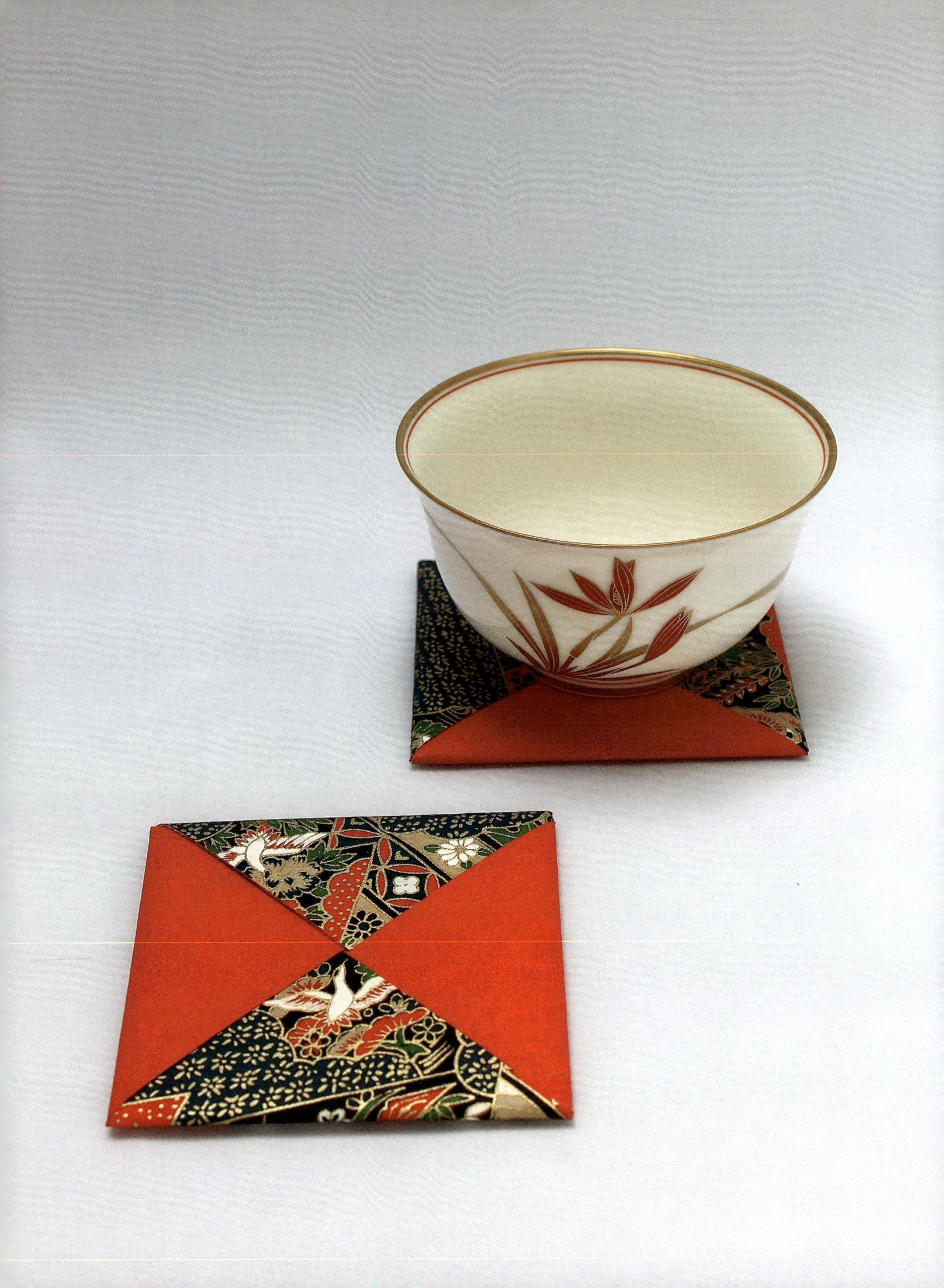

5

Fun Models

Cushioned Coaster

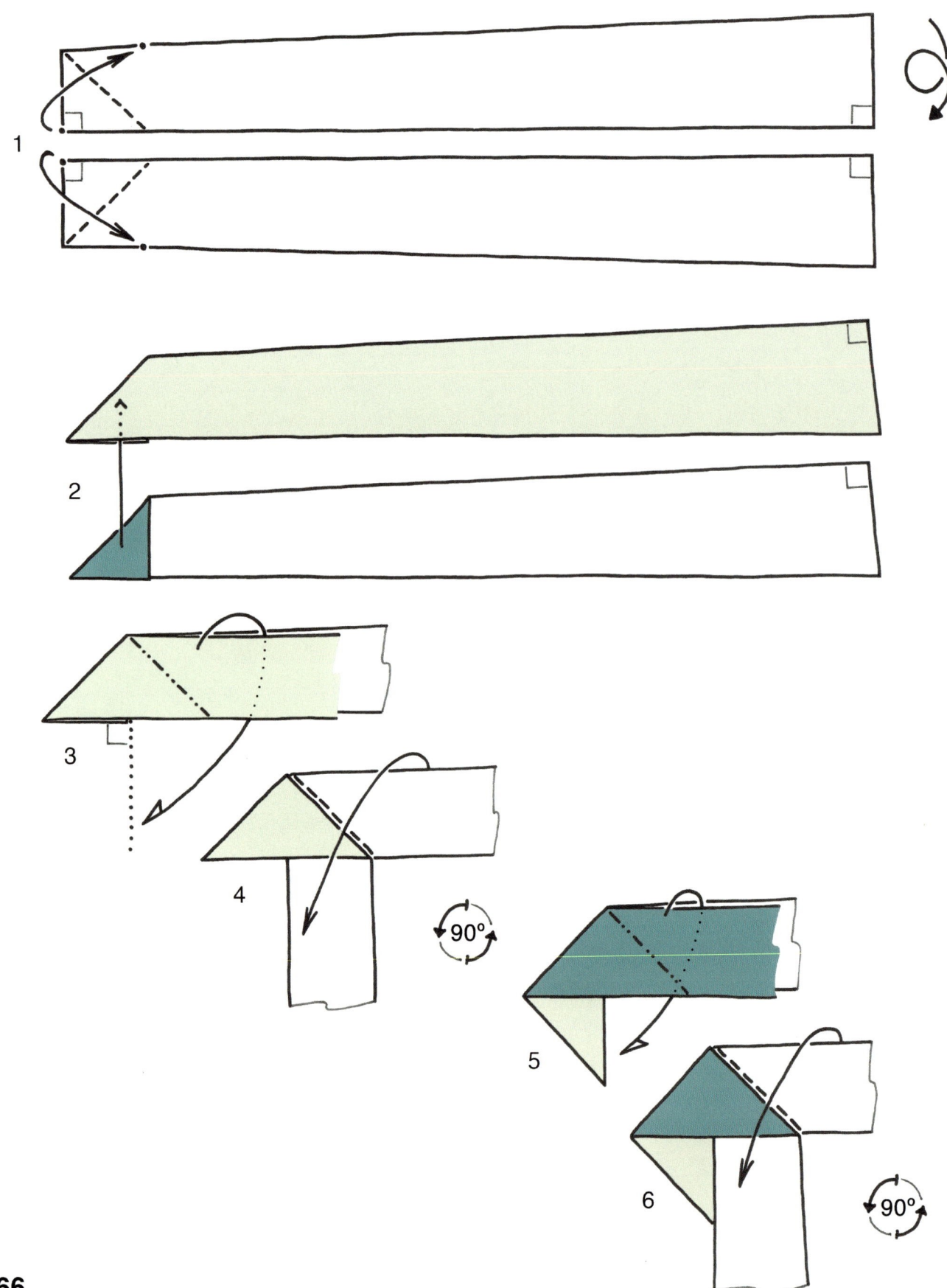

Use very gradually tapering strips, e.g. 100 x 6,0 x 5,5 cm will give a finished coaster 8,5 x 8,5 cm.

66

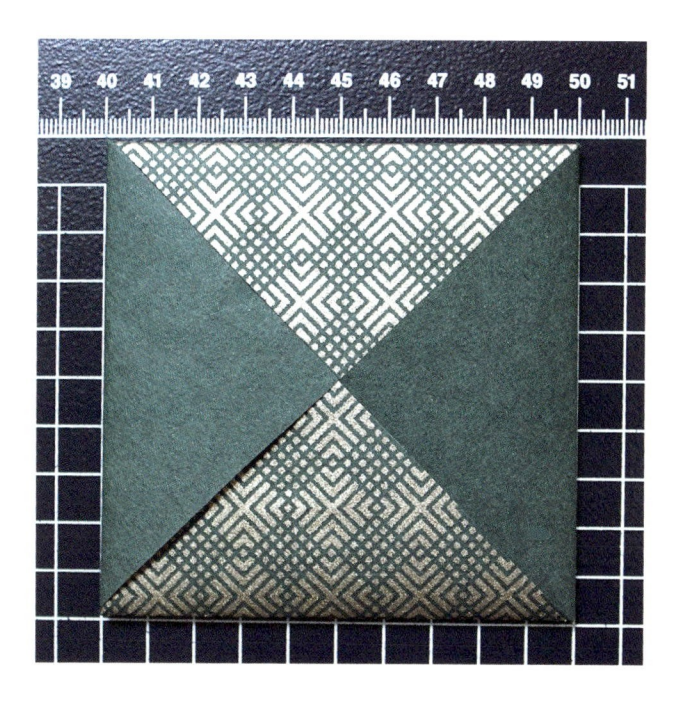

Step 7
The upper strip is folded behind the triangular corner.

Step 8
The rear strip is folded over the top.

Repeat steps 7 and 8. The upper strip folds behind the model and the rear strip folds in front, covering the layers like a pearl within an oyster.

Step 9
Only cut the upper strip.

The finished coaster is insulating and is highly suitable for tea lovers and thirsty cold beer drinkers alike!

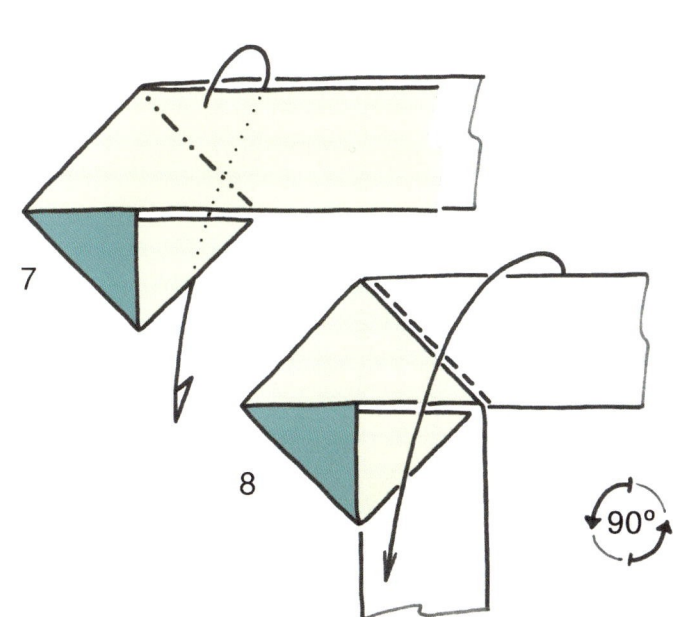

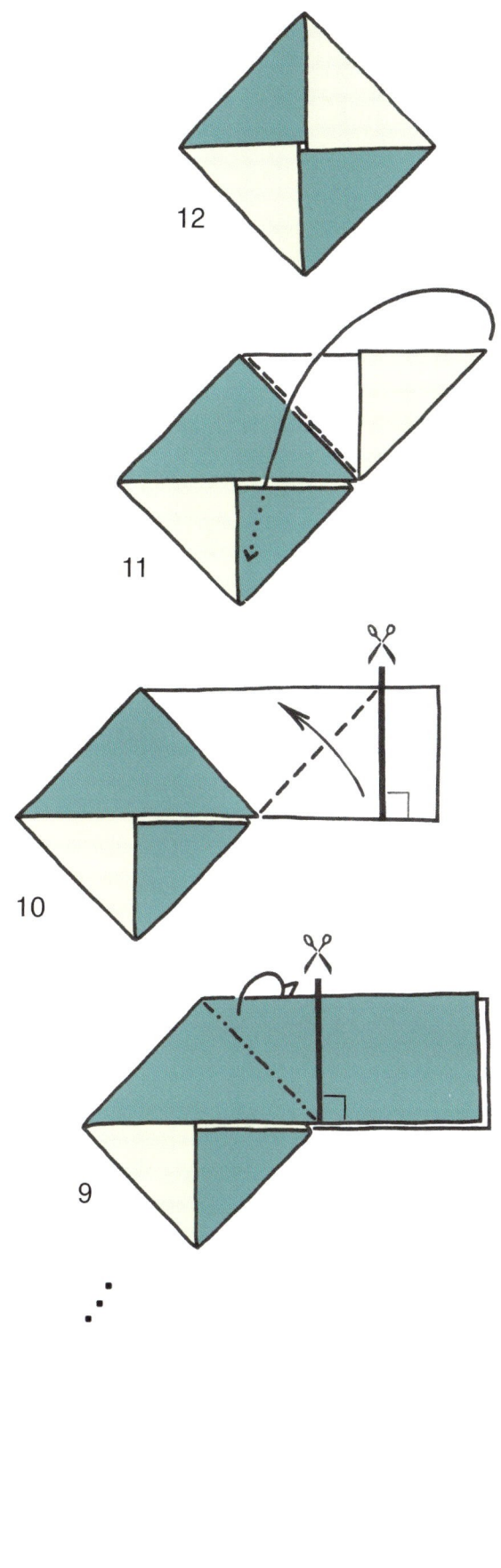

67

Puzzle Coaster

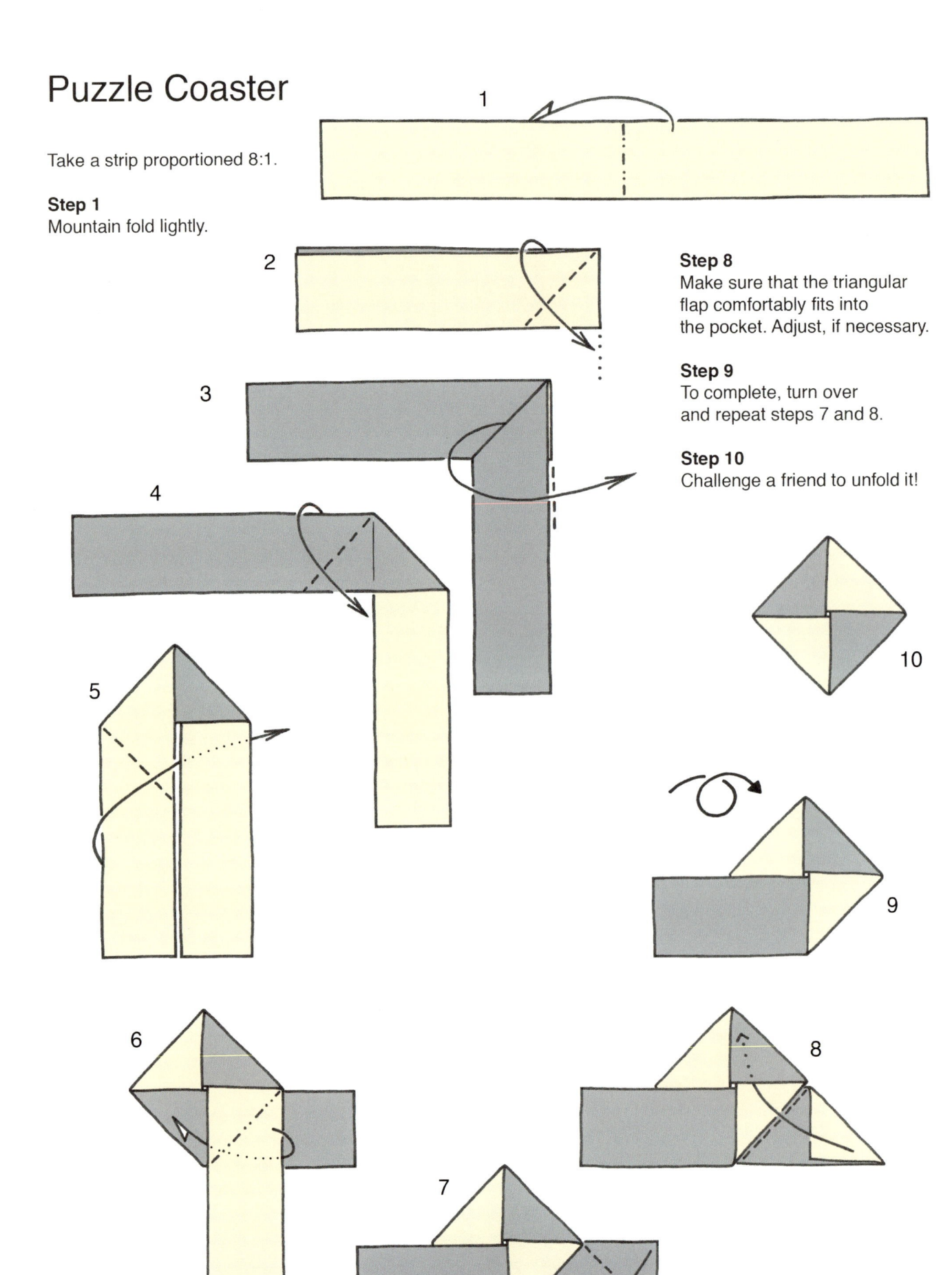

Take a strip proportioned 8:1.

Step 1
Mountain fold lightly.

Step 8
Make sure that the triangular flap comfortably fits into the pocket. Adjust, if necessary.

Step 9
To complete, turn over and repeat steps 7 and 8.

Step 10
Challenge a friend to unfold it!

68

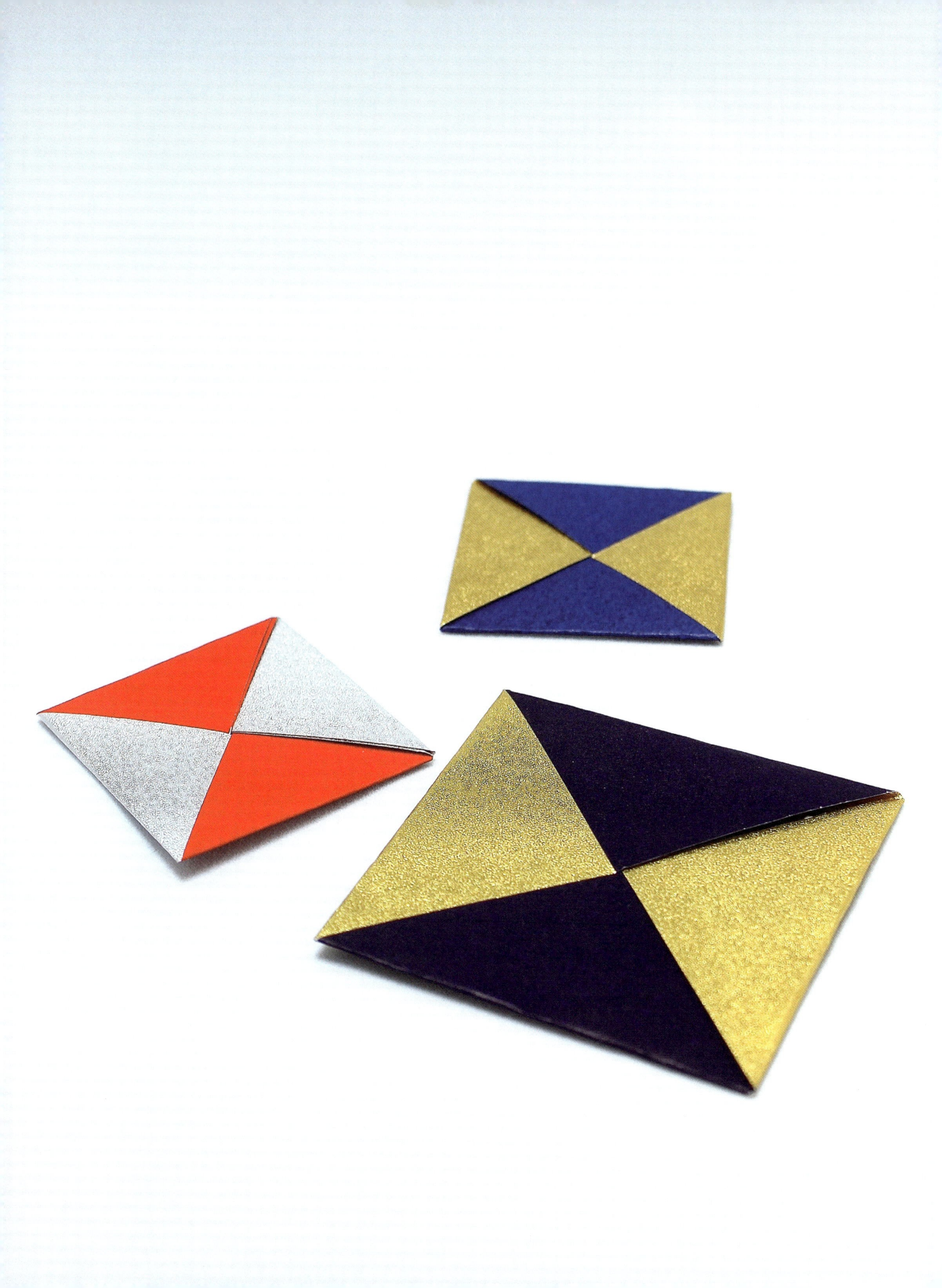

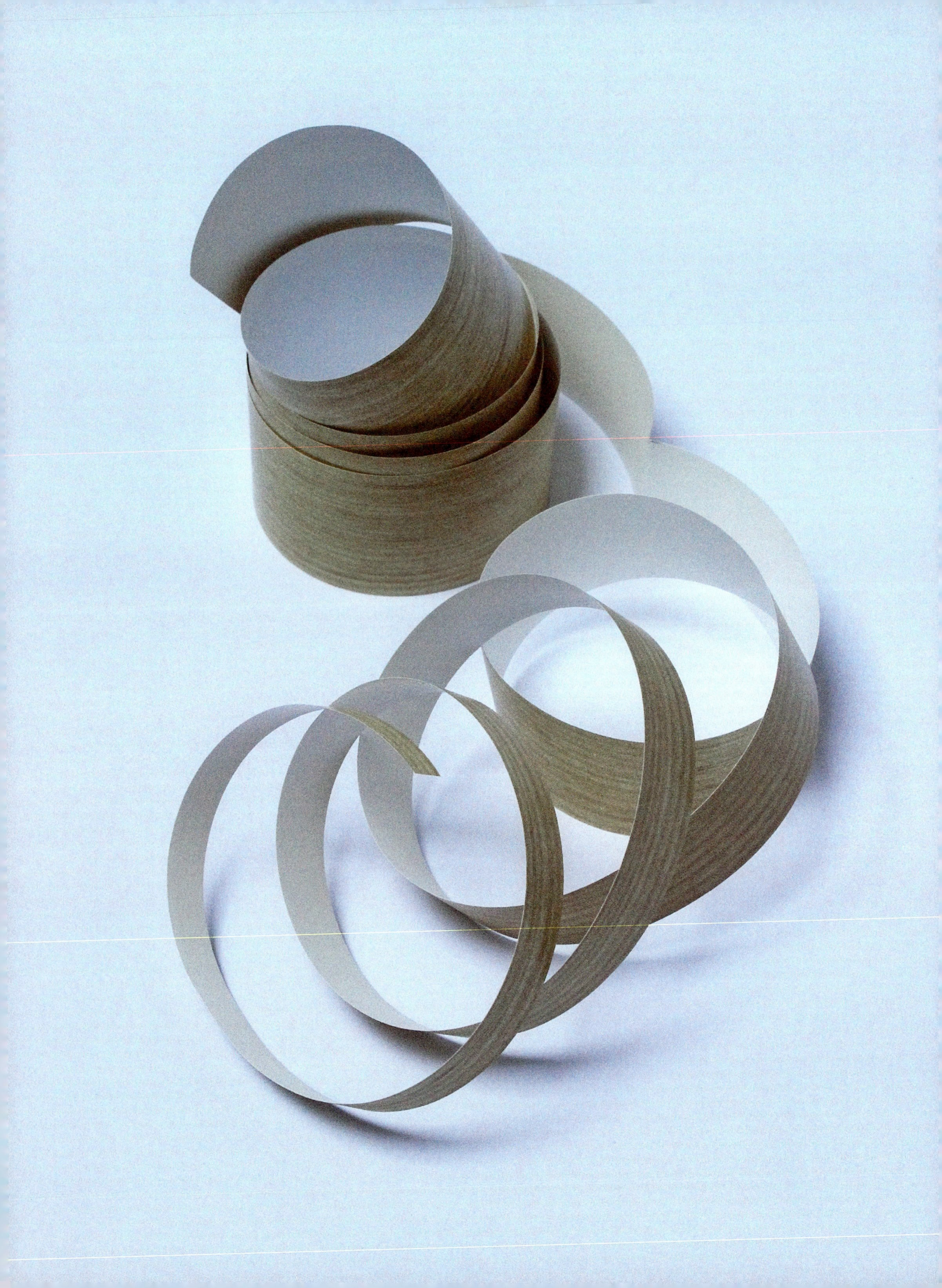

6

Easy ways to cut tapering strips

Some helpful tips

A key requirement for a perfect Curlicue is a precisely cut strip of paper. This section will help you to achieve it.

Aim for perfectly cut paper edges. You can use one of these methods:

- Best choice: paper trimmer machine (sometimes called a guillotine) with a cutting edge of at least 70 cm.
- Second best: long metal ruler, a cutting knife and a cutting mat.
- Very last resort: scissors and envelopener type cutting tools.

Hold the paper (or layers of paper) very firmly while cutting, to avoid inaccuracies caused by unintentional sliding of the paper (or the ruler).

Measure all sizes and mark all points accurately.

For easy handling, cut strips from a large sheet or roll of paper: it's very difficult to hold a small or narrow strip.

One possible material is gift-wrapping paper, which usually comes in rolls 70 cm wide. Trim the ready-cut edge, making sure that the corners are 90° and that the long sides are parallel.

Explanation of terms and symbols:
L - length of the paper strip (width of paper roll)
b - wide end of the strip
a - narrow end of the strip

A Curlicue can work with almost any size of strip. However, I recommend that you try this approximate ratio of lengths to widths:
L : b : a = 100 : 5 : 1
For example L x b x a = 100 x 5 x 1 cm or 60 x 3 x 0.6 cm … etc.

Generally the longer the strip, the better the result. This will give more layers, more corners and thus more beautiful patterns. Try 200 x 5 x 1 cm!

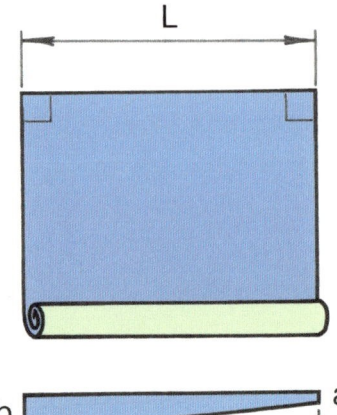

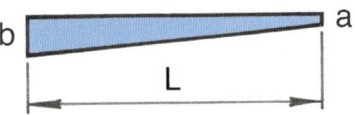

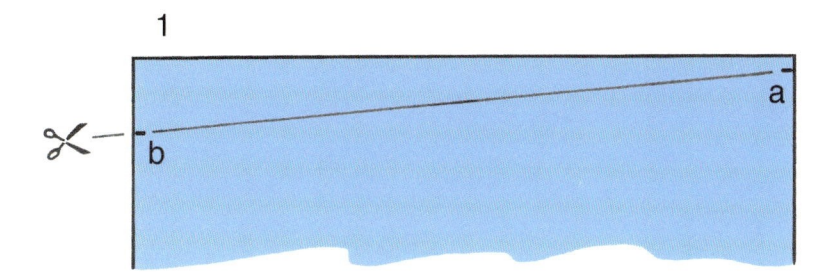

For example let's cut a strip with the following dimensions:
L = 70 cm, b = 5 cm, a = 1 cm .

Step 1
Work on the lighter side of the paper so that you can see the measuring marks. Use a sharp pencil to mark **a** and **b** on opposite sides. Connect **a** and **b** with a cut: there's no need to draw a line between them unless you have to use scissors or only have a short metal ruler.

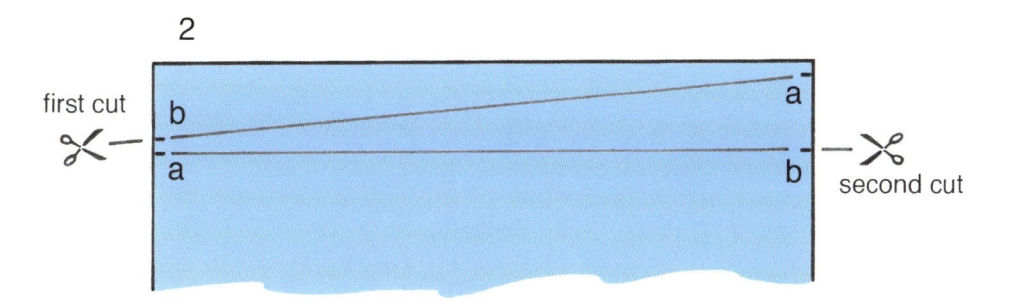

Step 2
To maintain a square edge on the roll, I recommend that you cut two identical strips every time. Mark the sides according to the diagram, and make the cuts in the order shown.

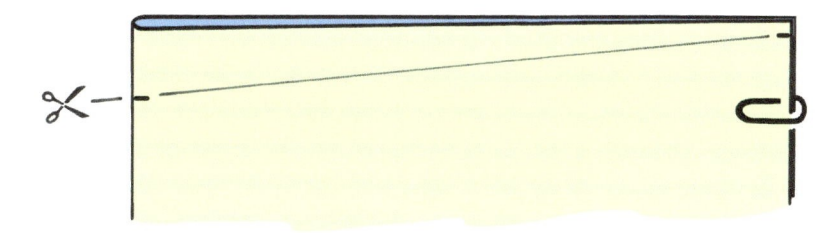

To obtain a double tapering strip first cut a rectangle from the roll measuring 140 cm x 70 cm (the width of the roll). Fold this in half to produce a double-thickness square 70 x 70 cm. Mark the sides according to the diagram and cut. Hold the layers together firmly during cutting by using paperclips or bulldog clips. This is shown by a paperclip symbol in these diagrams.

Cut a second doubled strip as described in step 2 to obtain a square edge.

Long strips

Here's a direct way to obtain a much longer tapering strip, e.g. L = 140 cm. Use a double thickness rectangle as described on page 73.
Example strip measurements: L = 140 cm, b = 5 cm, a = 1 cm.

Step 1
Make 3 marks **s** = 6 cm, where **s** is the sum of the small and wide ends of the strip: s = a + b, s = 1 cm + 5 cm.

Step 2
On the folded left hand edge make a central mark at **m**, where **m** is half way down to **s** (3 cm).

On the open right hand edges, make 2 marks, **a** on the front layer, **b** on the rear layer, each time measuring from the upper corners.

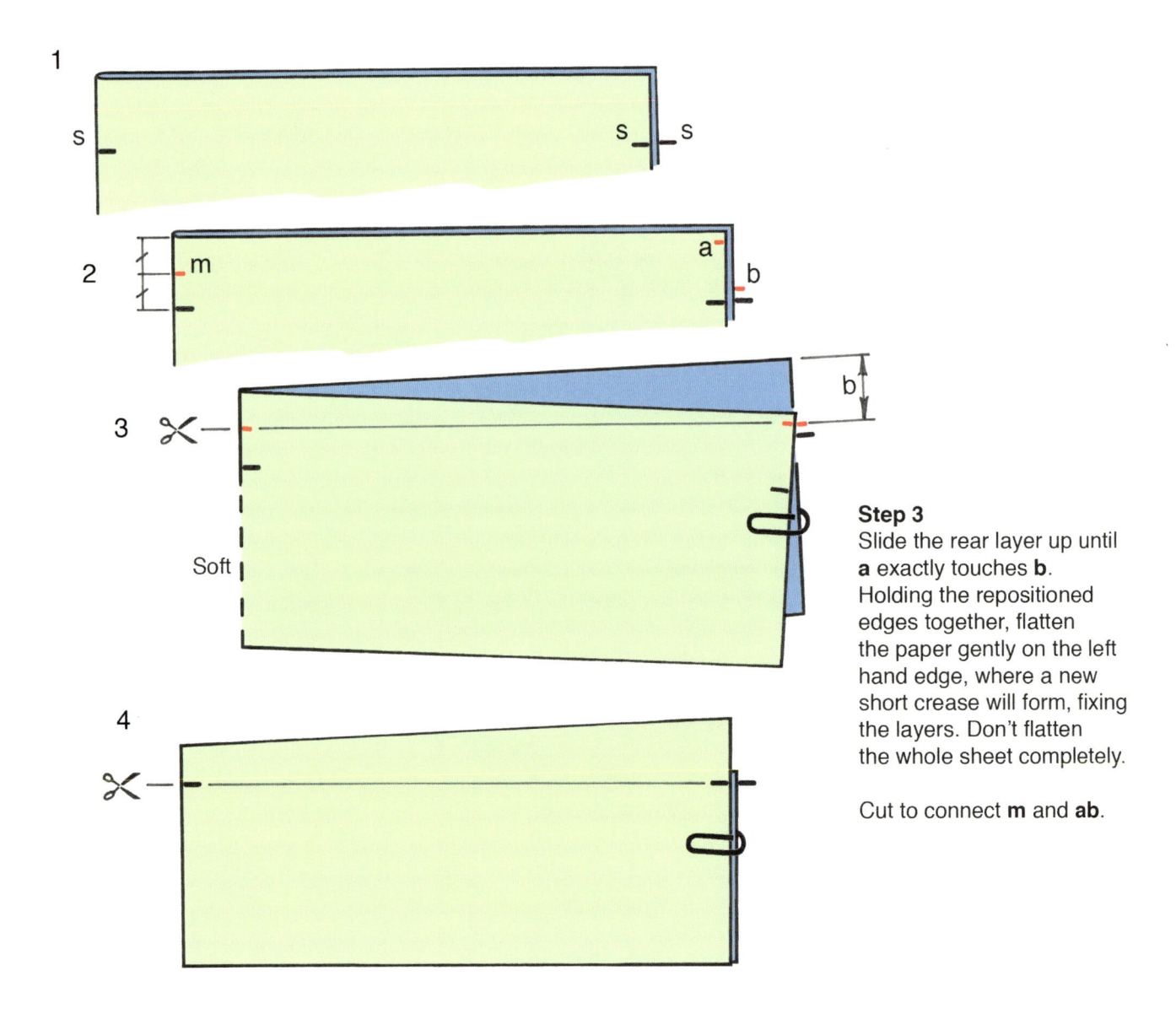

Step 3
Slide the rear layer up until **a** exactly touches **b**. Holding the repositioned edges together, flatten the paper gently on the left hand edge, where a new short crease will form, fixing the layers. Don't flatten the whole sheet completely.

Cut to connect **m** and **ab**.

Step 4
Slide the front layer back to its original position and make a second cut connecting **s** and **ss** to get a second strip.

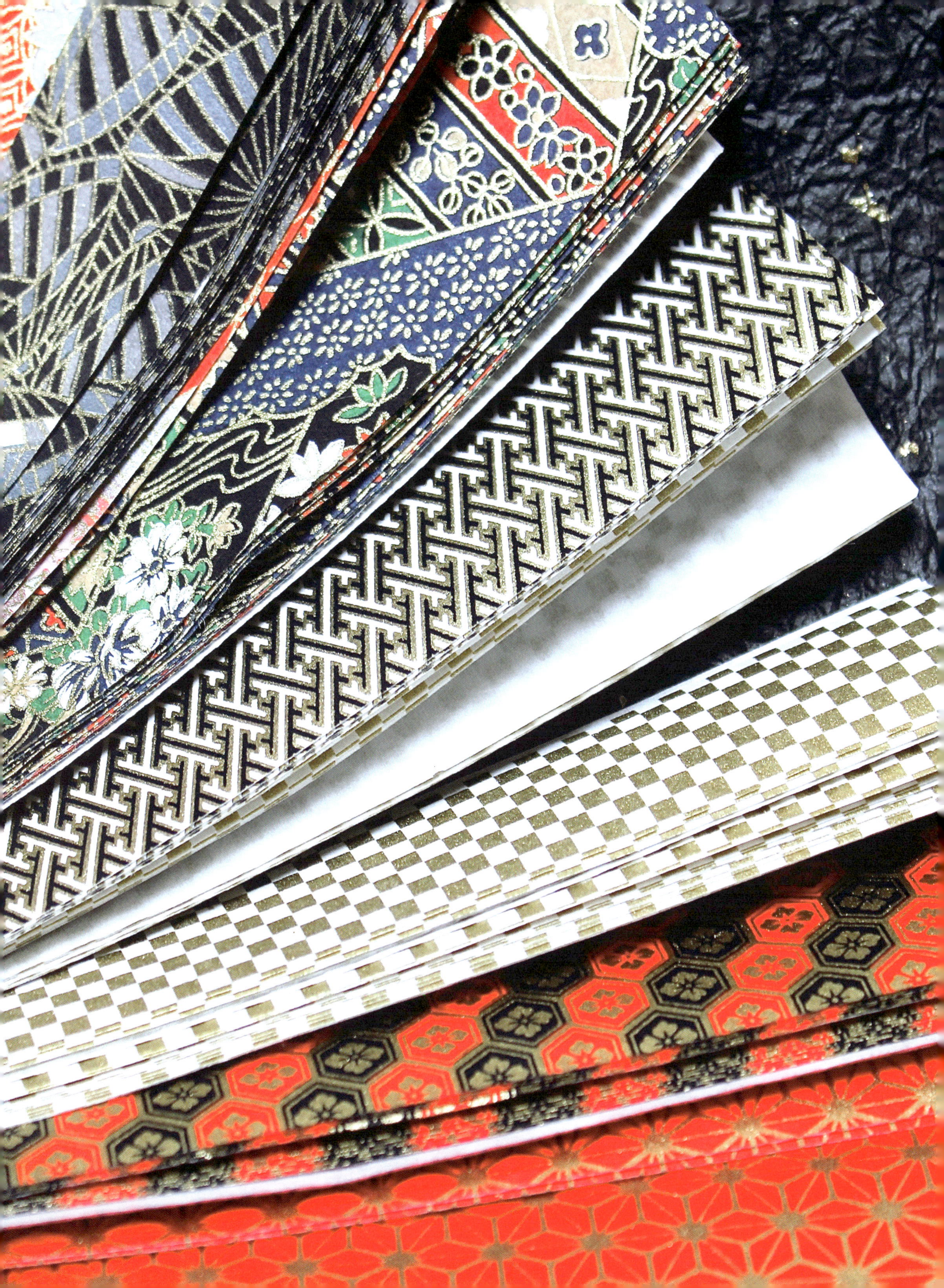

Acknowledgements

I should like to give my warmest and eternal thanks to all those who have played a part in this book. Firstly, my husband Dave with his origami experience and artist's eye, helped with all the stages of this book: its content, concept, text, and colour ideas. Dave has gently encouraged me to get on with the work. He helped me by cooking, by ironing, by buying me a camera and with his love.

My son Timur worked on layout, and taught me how to use Photoshop.
My proofreaders were Mark Robinson who painstakingly reviewed the text and made invaluable suggestions for stylistic improvements, and James Simon whose extensive origami knowledge was brought into play in folding and checking all my diagrams and sequences.
Himanshu Agrawal did some early proofreading and recommended CreateSpace on demand publishing.
Jeff Rutzky made many useful suggestions for improving the overall design as well as detailed text and style corrections.
Nick Robinson was invaluable with technical and computer support.

I must acknowledge the famous "trinity" of Ramin Razani, Paulo Bascetta and Herman Van Goubergen: during a late-night folding session in Freising, Germany, they suggested I should establish the originality of the Curlicue by publishing my work.
I thank Tomoko Fuse and Makoto Yamaguchi, the first real fans of the Curlicue, who actually wanted to publish it before me!
I also want to pay tribute to the wonderful work of Paulo Mulatinho and Silke Schröder whose Viereck Verlag publications were an almost daily inspiration.

Thank you to all of the above, and anyone else who has contributed in any way, small or large, in the development of the design and the production of this book.

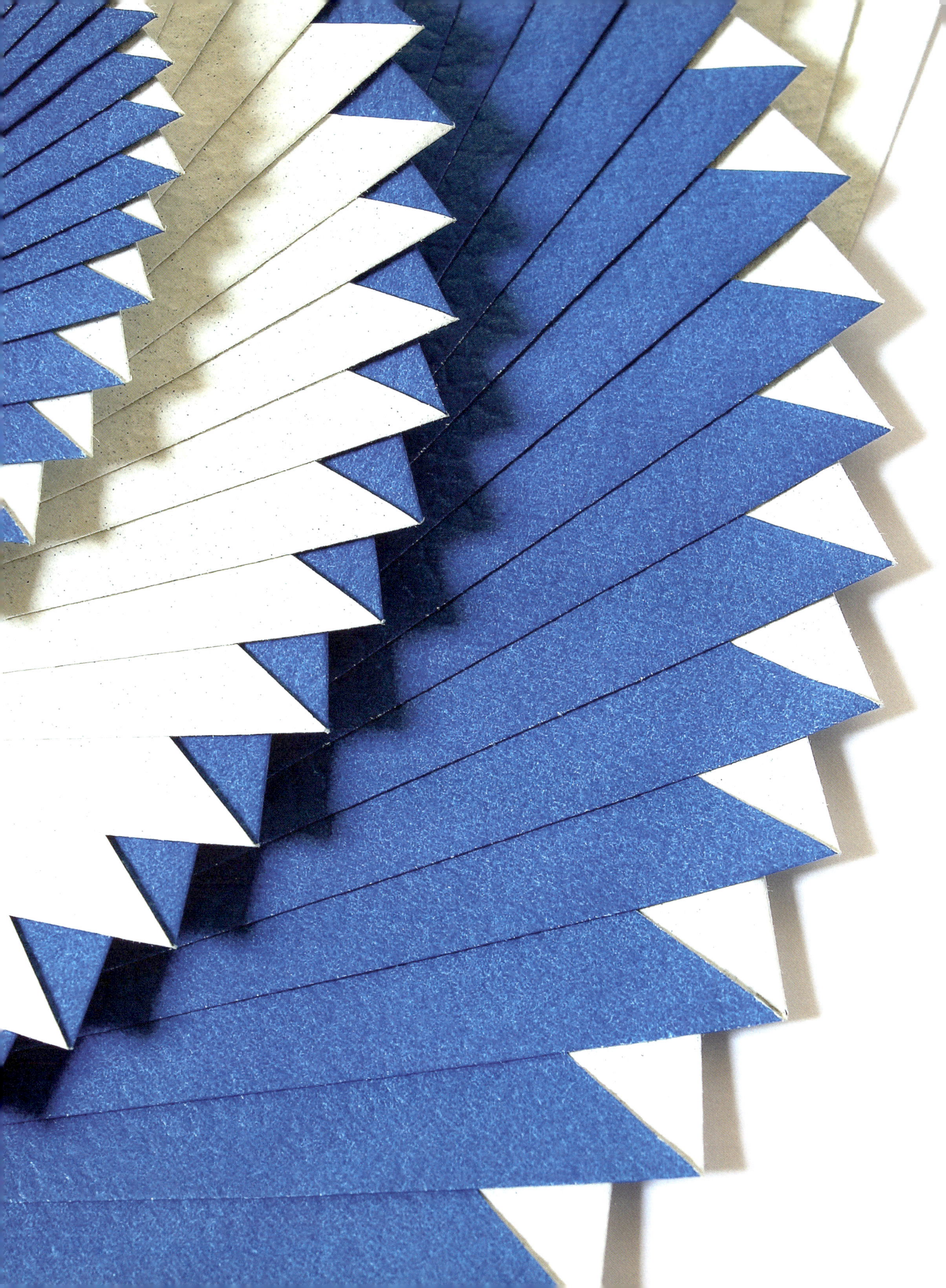

Postscript

There are many unexplored Curlicue variations, combinations and improvements, and it's now down to you to experiment! Please share with me what you discover.

You may be interested in the mass production of Curlicues as corporate gifts or toys: I have some detailed ideas about how this could be achieved using materials other than paper. If you feel you can contribute to this project, please contact me.

CPSIA information can be obtained at www.ICGtesting.com
Printed in the USA
LVIW01n1553180815
450602LV00006B/103